HEY, YOU!

Also by Michael Hollings
and published by Burns & Oates:

Purple Times

HEY, YOU!

by

MICHAEL HOLLINGS

LONDON
BURNS & OATES

Nihil Obstat: Georgivs Smith, s.t.d., ph.d. Censor Depvtatvs.
Imprimatvr: E. Morrogh Bernard, Vicarivs Generalis.
Westmonasterii: Die xxxi Decembris mcmliv.

Made and printed in Great Britain by
Billing & Sons Limited, Guildford, London and Worcester for
Search Press Limited, 2-10 Jerdan Place,
London SW6 5PT

CONTENTS

FOREWORD

THERE is danger everywhere! Danger from motor cars in the streets; death from bombs possible at any moment at one or two men's whim; danger from false philosophies eating like cancer into the universities, the schools, the daily newspapers; danger, dread. . . . Oh, let us forget it all and look at the TV.

Yes, the greatest danger is from ourselves. Because, though it has become quite fashionable to talk about God, to write about God, to quote the mystics, it is still very unfashionable to do much about it all. The original purpose of the articles which are here loosely sewn together to form a book was to point a finger at an average public. To point, and say that the business of knowing and loving God is not merely a theory, but a straight, plain and hard reality facing each one of us. God is everywhere, too, and much more truly than danger, much more powerfully. Now, the prophets of old had to stand in the cities or in the desert literally shouting about repentance—active, vital, personal. They rent their garments and put ashes on their heads.

And the people did not listen. . . .

When Christ came, the story was just the same. . . .

Today there is no difference, unless it is that there is more speed and less ability to listen. It will be the same tomorrow, and till the end of time.

But today instead of the prophets, Christ has left the priests with a duty as great as the prophets. He has left them not only the message of God to deliver. He has given them the very life of God to hand on through the Sacraments.

To face this responsibility, the priest is given grace. He has to become more and more identified with the work of the one High Priest, Christ. He has to become in some sense a victim

7

to share the daily sacrifice of Christ at Mass. All his prayer, all the liturgy, all his life must face the Cross, whether he likes it or not.

The danger of the priest is that he may "know all the answers". In knowing the answers he may do little or nothing about them. Yet his salvation and that of his people is in facing, carrying, being nailed to the Cross.

The difficulty? To line theory up with practice. He must somehow teach those with whom he is in contact to know, love and serve God. He must make them see that they are called to be future saints—not anyone else, not in theory only, but here and now, a future saint—YOU. This is Christianity. The path to heaven, which is the path of the sinner who is to be a saint, this path begins at once, and is a very ordinary, rutted path. It is daily life at work, at home, in church, in a bad temper, in deep peace, in wretched pain, in poverty or in Park Lane. Those who read what I had written were unwise enough to say that the material helped them practically in this purpose; that, after reading, they could go away, urged to follow a deeper life of prayer. They said they wanted others to read, so that they could go and make the same effort.

There is no point, then, in reading further unless you are prepared to do something practical. What does that mean? It means that, by prayer, by going to Mass and Communion, by reading into the liturgy, you are ready to grow more fully in the love and service of God.

If you read, you will find some parts are staccato, some loud, some even offensive. I make no apologies, because few can see the limitations more clearly than I do. In allowing the book to go ahead, I can only suppose that the more one tries to love God, the more incredible it becomes that he should use such odd methods to achieve his will, which is, you know,

I

GETTING DOWN TO PRAYER

I

HEY, YOU!

Hey, you! Yes! *You!* Get things straight! *Be* what you are always talking about. Leaven the world. Start praying. *Now!*

I am going to tell you about the most important thing in your life and mine, and if I sound a bit noisy it's because I have to make myself heard above the din of typewriters, wireless, jet aircraft and mankind in general. And I ask you to listen because it's vital for you in the true sense of the word.

When I say . . . what's that? You can't waste time reading this now? You're off to catch the tube? A civil servant, I suppose? Oh, working in the city. Well, take this along with you, because what I am going to say will shatter the city to its foundations, and the civil service, and the other professions!

I am telling you to pray more.

I am telling you prayer is the keystone of your life.

I am telling you to be a saint.

That will shake them!—All the men with bowler hats and rolled umbrellas, all the men who have no hats and no umbrellas; all the terribly serious, long-haired young men in universities, all the nice empty-headed young men everywhere; all the tall and short, whether brainy or brawny, dull, religious, agnostic; all the sports fiends, the jazz fiends, the talkers; those who sit silent, those who are not so young as they used to be, who have lost the first enthusiasm; the artists and the critics of art; scientists and those who pride themselves on being able to think; all the halt and maimed, rich and poor, perverts, neurotics, introverts, extraverts, idlers, intellectuals, workers, sinners—children of God—You!

You must pray!

You must develop spiritually.

What is this all about and why do I insist on it so vehemently?

Because it is all very nice to have magazines and programmes and study circles and action, societies and sodalities. It is very good, very necessary, very admirable. It means you may have to work very hard. You have to chase people up. It takes a lot of money and time, with "sales talks" and organization. But is there not something more behind it all, the vital spring which puts life into what we are doing? Prayer.

Why? That depends what the object is; where we are heading. Where are we heading anyhow?—Can it be we are sometimes a little vague, losing ourselves in the doing on one side, or the theory disconnected from the practice on the other?

Now, you armchair critic, it is your turn now. What is the aim and object of our planning? To re-educate our brethren? Chatty essays by distinguished or undistinguished authors on topics of varying interest? Book reviews? Excellent! Anything else?

Oh! Someone said something about being a soldier of Christ. Can you define that? A soldier is not much good unless he has weapons, unless he is trained. He should have spirit and discipline and something to urge him into battle. That is an ordinary one. But a soldier of Christ needs more still. He is not trying to slaughter his opponents with machine-gun logic or atomizing arguments. He can only win the war by winning men. He must be magnetic.

He sets about the winning of men through the lay apostolate. Very well! But that phrase is barren to you unless you are an apostle. You will go off with the fizz of a damp squib and not the reverberation of a magnetic mine, if you are not an apostle. For to be an apostle you must be burning and brimming over with the love of God. What does this love mean? It means sowing the seed of prayer from which love grows, prayer which means sacrifice, humiliation; it means giving the utmost, and then giving a little more. It means *being* more than *doing*. Love means the Agony in the Garden and then the Way of the Cross; it means crucifixion and death long before there is any resurrection and ascension.

How do you feel about that? Suffering! Failure! All right as a theory, ' imagine. Supposing, though, that it touches you. So many of our theories work out imperceptibly into terms of success. Failure is not considered personally. Discussion ends in discussion. If your apostolate is careering round organizing, you will probably burn yourself out, unless cooled by prayer. If your apostolate is from an armchair, with your feet up, the only thing you are likely to set on fire is your carpet, when you doze and drop your cigarette. Yet Christ said, "I came to cast fire upon the earth, and what would I but that it be kindled".

Your enthusiasm will not last long if it is only borrowed from a book. You will soon droop if you do not pray. Furthermore, you will not encourage anyone to go about the world loving God, if you are not leading the way, a pillar of fire in materialist darkness.

Pro eis sanctifico meipsum.   For them do I sanctify myself.

The phrase has rightly been made into the key of the apostolate. But what is the effect of it on each individual? Does it penetrate our lives? What does it make us do? Weekday Mass, on and off? More prayer? The Rosary? All of this or some of it, a bit scrappy, a bit damped by waning enthusiasm. For fanaticism is not right! People do not understand it. Anyhow, there is the rest of our life to lead, the job, the essential relaxation. There is so little time to spare, and when you think that we do perform more than a great many—

well, it is not bad. And—yes, there is prayer whenever possible, and not much more can be taken on without fear of cracking up.

I know, I *know*, I *know!* We have had it all out over and over again. But it will and must always come back to this. Prayer is the power of the apostolate, prayer is the life of your work. Prayer drives, prayer encourages, prayer humbles; prayer learns patience; prayer is the teacher, the channel, the expression of love. Without prayer, whatever springs from you will not flourish, any more than a tree will without roots. Unless you can see this—no, unless you can appreciate it sufficiently to practise prayer—you are in grave danger of wasting your energy. Theoretical understanding is not enough. You must force the idea into the depth of your brain, and when it is ensconced there with no danger of it being camouflaged or littered-up, then you can plan your action. Because then the first action will be always to pray; and the last action will be to pray; so that the action in between will be prayer in action, which must never be allowed to deteriorate into action without prayer.

Have you got it firmly fixed in your mind, with something more active than mere acknowledgement? Are you already saying we know all this and have been doing exactly this for years? Or perhaps you are saying this man is mad, and knows nothing of Catholic Action or the lay Apostolate or prayer. You may well be right. But that would not change my emphasis. No one wants you to be a tub-thumper; no one wants you to be a big business organizer. But if you are these things, then get down on your knees and beg God's grace that you may use your talent in doing his will. No one suggests that you are a contemplative monk, living in the world, but there is every reason why you should be a contemplative. God does not care whether you lick stamps in an office, or dig ditches in the country, or run the Bank of

England. He wants to use you, and he can use you. But he can only use you in his way and not in yours. If you are charging ahead worldliwise, and are getting God organized you should readjust your method slightly. Péguy makes God say of man:

> But what you cannot ask of him, by gum, is a little hope.
> A little confidence, don't you know, a little relaxation.
> A little yielding, a little abandonment into my hands,
> A little giving in, he is always so stiff.[1]

Now prayer is just that, is just the cure for that. It sets God as the keystone of your work, forgetting your powers and your plans for God's plan—God's plan which you will never see more than darkly in this world, but which you will never see at all, if you are busy looking at yourself.

You have to be sanctified, made a saint, in order that God can use you. You must be tempered, and there is no easy way of tempering. For any way chosen is the way of the Cross, if it is the right way, whatever name you may call it, whatever habit or uniform you may wear. Yet the call is there to draw us. That is simple. The way is there; that is simple too. St Teresa of Avila commented that if anyone said there was another way to perfection, except through prayer, he was wrong.

What is the long and short of this outpouring? I am supposed to be writing about prayer; you are supposed to be glancing at what I have written. But glancing alone is not enough. We can talk of the mechanics of prayer, and how to pray and where and why. But the main necessity must be to impress forever the conviction—the active and effective conviction—that all your gifts without sanctity are useless, while in reverse, sanctity alone will win the world to follow Christ.

[1] 'Abandonment' from God Speaks, tr. by Julian Green (Pantheon Books Inc.).

This is for you! Not for anyone else you can think of whom it would suit—it is for you!

Now—go to it! Go to pray! When you are tired, pray the longer. It will seem endless, a useless waste of time. Excellent; for you could not be wasting it in a better way. *Oremus!*

II

WHAT AND WHY

CATECHISM classes!

Who made you?—God made me.

To a Catholic in childhood, there probably was not much significance in the answer, except that the failure to get it right might mean a penalty. In this, at least, a convert gains! For the connection between this question and our lives is—or should be—basic to our behaviour. Remove it, and there is no faith, and no necessity for morals. Ignore it, and you can think yourself your own master until you are knocked down by a bus or told you have an incurable disease. Accept it, and the kaleidoscope reveals a pattern. It is basic because it gives each man a relationship to God.

How do you behave towards your family? You are a funny kind of son if you proudly proclaim you have not, and never had, a father. Stranger still if you live in your father's house and never speak to him. Prayer is speaking to your father. Prayer is speaking to God. Prayer is living with your father, God. Unfortunately it does not seem to us to be as simple as that. In praying we are either at the awkward age when we shift uneasily from one foot to the other, search desperately for things to say and long for the interview to end; like the boy on the mat before his father we long to get away and go on playing with our lives. Or else we are too grown up and independent to understand that a father's interest remains centred in his son, when the child's mind has already wandered to what it thinks are more absorbing occupations.

There is nothing more absorbing than prayer, because

prayer uses the whole man. Prayer is the raising of man's mind to God. Prayer is the raising of man's heart to God. Prayer is the adoration of man's body before God. What does the raising of the mind to God mean? How can we begin to do it? It means that our minds move naturally upon a natural level. Beginning the day, we are immersed in our immediate predicament; we must get to the office, but first we must eat something; we must attend a parade or get the rations; we are troubled about the chance of rain next Saturday; we are married, about to marry, worried that we are not married, or engrossed in being single. We swim in it all, the sea of everyday joys, cares, parties, games, food, health. To move our thoughts from this level, quite literally we must raise them. Reading a murder story comes more easily to most of us than translating Euripides. Even in human matters there are different levels. And therefore it is reasonable to think that an effort is necessary to raise the mind to thoughts about God.

God is a spirit: man is matter and spirit. God is: man depends. God is infinite: man is finite. Left to himself man cannot climb the intellectual heights of prayer. He puts finite against the infinite and it does not work out. He makes an effort; it is beyond his strength. He can come by unaided reason to know that God exists. He cannot come by reason alone to know God. This helplessness hurts man's pride, as Dryden says:

> *Thus man by his own strength to heaven wou'd soar,*
> *And wou'd not be obliged to God for more.*

We cannot hope to pray like that. In the act of raising the mind we can go only so far, and even then need God's help from start to finish. In this world, we do not reach the Beatific Vision, which is the fullest knowledge of Infinite God possible to finite man. The mind reaches outward and upward, ever developing, seeking God; or, bored, tired, distracted, it gives up the struggle. There is something it cannot grasp, because that Something is too big; so the mind sees flashes of awful truth, and then subsides again into plunging darkness.

Therefore, in this world it is more important to love God than to know him.

That is not mere wordiness. That is the teaching of the Angelic Doctor. For that reason, we must raise the heart as well as the mind. We cannot understand, but we cannot stop short. We must go beyond understanding. We must cling with the will. Before anything, we must kneel with the will. And so, prayer is largely the battle of the will; its lower self would like to be tucked up in bed, while its higher self demands a struggle through the act of contrition, kneeling on the bare boards or piled carpet. The heart too is being raised up. What is this raising up? It is a constant pressure, a constant leaning forward like the tapping stick of a blind man. The will is a blind faculty. While it can touch, it is full of confidence. When the pavement falls away, when the stick, beating wildly on air, is answered by silence, blind groping may become a panic. Reason guiding the heart says "Stop"; the heart drawn beyond understanding answers "Go on". It does not understand, it only knows it must go on.

Do you see anything of the nature of prayer emerging from this? What has been said should not be altogether obscure. On the other hand, these words are only signs, pointers to the meaning of prayer. The raising of the mind and heart to God automatically implies the humbling of the mind and heart before God. God made me. Here is cause enough for humility. Kneeling is the attitude of prayer *par excellence*. And the more we kneel, the more we shall grow in humility, because we shall realize how little we realize, understand how little our heart is in our prayer.

The complete man, then, is occupied by prayer—his body bent before God's majesty, his mind trained towards his frail idea of God, his will grasping at the will of God, which is love. All this is so, because his nature demands recognition of his creator, however much his lower nature may rebel at the act of recognition. *Laborare est orare. Orare est laborare.*

Not without justification is it said that prayer is the first of the eminent good works. Prayer is hard work, and though he can grow in the art, like a learner heaving a bale of cotton, the more man prays, the less feeling of satisfaction he derives. First he is full of enthusiasm, soon he grows weary. God withdraws. He is alone. He gets up and goes for a walk. Why is prayer so difficult and why so dull?

It is not! That is the only answer. But sometimes we forget why we are praying—praying to give adoration, glory and thanks to God. Not for a smug glow of self-satisfaction! *Laudate Dominum omnes gentes.* God is the object of our prayer. True, we must ask and we shall receive, but asking is only a section of praying, it is not the end in itself. If we are seeking merely our selfish consolation, we are not praying in the right way. Yet, if we seek God, we shall find consolation, though it should be in the utter desolation of getting nowhere.

Is this all rather in the air; not very practical? Of course it is! This is the theory of prayer, and you cannot get anywhere just by looking at a theory. Prayer itself is eminently practical, because it is making use of the whole man to put him in touch with God. It is occupying all man's time and all man's energy. Not only on Sundays, not only on his knees does a man pray. There he lays the foundation, he and God working together in silence. Everything else is given up temporarily. Man is no longer running away. "Be still and see that I am God." God is the sole object. But no one suggests that it would be the will of God for all mankind to be in adoration all day long, literally kneeling before the tabernacle. Man must live by

the sweat of his brow. That sweat, however, glorifies God,
that panting breath praises God, that roughened hand is
lifted in salutation to God. By seeking God on his knees, man
grows able to carry him in his mind and heart throughout
his life.

If, then, you have read this far, it is time for theory to drive
you to practice. Knowing leads to loving. The intellect yields
place to the will. God is your tutor. Go—and talk to God.
But you do not know what to say? Listen to a Carmelite nun:
"I do as a child would who cannot read—I say just what I
want to say to God, quite simply, and he never fails to understand."

"Go thou and do likewise!"

III

TALKING THINGS OVER

If it is difficult to begin to pray, it is more difficult to explain to someone else how to begin to pray. Of course, there are those who do nothing else but talk about it, and never get down to praying. That is not the point. Again and again the truth must be repeated. You and I are only going to learn by practice; knowledge of prayer is a practical knowledge. Is it useless for any man to try to teach another the way of prayer? No, because God has a practice himself, the practice of using one man to help another. It is not essential, but it is usual. It is the lesson of the history of revelation, it is the use of the spoken and written word, it is finally the use of the Word of God, the Word made flesh. Therefore. . . . "Lord, teach us to pray. . . ."

The apostles went to the source of knowledge for an answer about praying. We can do no better. Christ did this mysterious thing—praying. In some way, it seemed to be connected with everything else that was different in him, setting him apart from other men. Christ went to pray before he preached. He went to pray after he preached. He went to pray before healing, before teaching, before miracles. And somehow it did not seem drudgery. The apostles did not shrink from it, but begged for it. It gave refreshment; it was a tonic, so to speak, which gave Christ new vigour at the end of a tiring day or before some big work. Because it gave Christ new vigour, it would give them new vigour if they could imitate him. Like master, like man. Prayer had this subtle connection in their eyes with the "secret" of Christ's "success".

22

Later, they saw that it was a basic part of his doctrine, as of his practice. St Matthew therefore placed the prayer passage into the sermon on the mount.

"When you pray you shall not be as the hypocrites. . . ." Christ is very matter-of-fact in his teaching. He sets the stage for prayer. Before dealing with what must be said, there is great importance attached to the way in which it is to be said. Prayer to a large extent is an attitude of mind and heart. It is worse than useless to pray simply because it is expected of us, from our position in life. It is worse than useless, degrading, to pray simply in order to draw attention "as the hypocrites that love to stand and pray in synagogues and corners of the street that they may be seen by men" . . . or go to Sunday Mass because it is "done" (what would the neighbours say if we did not?); or acknowledge God when he is popular, and ignore him when business, politics or society show the lead; go to Mass in Ireland, lie abed in England; pray in school, drop it off at home. This is hardly worthy of the name of prayer, whatever man calls it when he does it. That motive of human respect is wrong. That is being a hypocrite, and being a hypocrite nullifies the prayer before it is begun.

The secret of prayer lies in the heart; the secret is between man and God. Real prayer is always private, however public it may be. Your chamber and the closed door to it may shut you within four walls and you may still be public if neon lights proclaim that you are in prayer and must not be disturbed. Whereas in the most crowded cathedral or market place, difficult as it may seem, you may still be alone with God, in secret prayer. "Out of the heart the mouth speaketh." So said Christ, and his other words follow logically.

"When you are praying, speak not much. . . ." This might seem a condemnation of vocal prayer, rather than what it is in fact, an introduction to the way of vocal prayer. It was necessary for Christ to get a further clear idea into the heads of the apostles. Normally, the beginning of prayer may be tongue-tied; but often it becomes garrulous. The apostles did not know how to talk to God, so they asked Christ.

Man does not know how to start, but once begun, he may be afraid to stop using words in case, as he thinks, he will in that way lose what contact he has made. He becomes obsessed by words, which can help, but also hinder his approach to God. The heathen—"they think in their much speaking they may be heard"—reel off an endless series of set prayers, a mere chemical formula working out to make something pleasing to God; indeed, the prayer wheel of the East shows how the formula may go on developing at so many thousand turns or prayers a minute, while the busy chemist-prayer gets on with another job. But the ordinary chemist can be uninterested, can even hate his job, yet still get the formula to work out. Not so the man at prayer. Man praying must have his heart behind his words. Words alone are dead. Words never please God if they are empty; they must hold man's heart within them.

However beautiful a turn of phrase, however perfect a soliloquy, however long-winded a prayer, it is "as sounding brass and tinkling cymbal" without charity, love, the expression of the heart. For the heart when it pours forth its love may do so in many words; but more often it does so in few, in repeated phrases like the couple whose love spoke thus: "Darling," said the man. "Yes, darling?" said the woman. "Nothing, darling," said the man, "Only darling, darling!" God knows it all before man says it. God loves it all before man says it. God is loving man for saying it, not the words, but man. The words may be nonsense; words of love often are nonsense. That is why it is important that man should sometimes say his own words in prayer, not always the beautiful words of someone else, which do not spring from within him; which express nothing on his tongue, because they do press out from his heart. One word of love, one silent glance of love, these exceed whole books of prayers read with dry meaningless unthinking.

"Thus therefore shalt thou pray: Our Father. . . ." Here man faces up to prayer! He asked how to pray, and God has taught him. First he taught the disposition; now the words. Not many words; but they are important words. Words which cover every aspect of man's relationship to God—they crowd in; fatherhood, man's next of kin; faith, hope and charity, acts that are directed immediately to God, fulfilling the purpose of man's creation; petition, the child asking its father for all the things it needs, food, loving kindness, happy security. A few words, sufficient for less than a minute or more than a lifetime of prayer. Here man finds the sure backing of God for vocal prayer. Therefore, let no man despise it, no man grow too big for it. Vocal prayer has the finger of God pointing it out; it was used by Christ till the end. Vocal prayer is the basic prayer, the foundation of all other kinds of prayer, the spring-board to which the diver comes back between his plunges into the depth. Without it, man will not learn to pray, prayer will not be complete. Though time and practice and above all the grace of God modify the number and kind of words man uses, words remain through life, to help in uniting man to God.

The Mass is a sacrifice, it is a vocal prayer. The Divine Office, *opus Dei*, bound upon priests and religious by the Church, is a vocal prayer. The "Our Father", best of all prayers, says the Catechism, is a vocal prayer. Though the apostles may not have realized it, they had already made a vocal prayer when they said "Lord, teach us to pray". What clearer example can we want of the teaching of our Lord? And because he is God, he does not deceive us in his teaching. To each man, vocal prayer must be a duty carried on in life, passing even through death in the vision of St John of the court of heaven, as the bell at Mass reminds us: *Sanctus, sanctus, sanctus,* Lord God Almighty!

Now, get out the New Testament, and read St Matthew vi and St Luke xi. The doctrine of prayer comes from the Gospel. It is clear and concise. Indeed, words written here cannot clarify, for man's duty is plain. Watch and pray. Man must accept what Christ taught and get on with it. The Church is at hand to guide. Therefore, no man is at liberty to say he cannot pray. The disposition necessary has been pointed out, the words have been set and handed down. Man must go ahead. He may begin with the sign of the Cross, continue with "Our Father", fill out his prayer by "Hail Mary" and finish with the sign of the Cross. If he does this, regularly, dutifully, lovingly, with patience in humility, with perseverance in boredom, willing even though not understanding, living the prayer of his living lips, so that his prayer is living and he is living in prayer. . . . If he does this, he has begun upon the path of prayer. That path leads to heaven. No other path does. Because of this, the path is the way of the Cross. That is logical.

A man in prayer says "Our Father, thy will be done". The act of the will is love. Christ said to come after him, man must take up his cross daily. Love and the Cross unite in the words of Christ, the words of prayer, and the life of Christ in man. This follows because Christ is leading us. His greatest prayer was the prayer of the Cross, which was in part made up of vocal prayer. All man's prayer turns on the imitation of Christ, for the servant is not greater than the master. Wishing then to learn something of prayer, beginning to know something of vocal prayer, man turns to God in the only way he knows, raising his mind and heart, expressing himself by posture and by word of mouth . . . man, apostle, disciple, lost or strayed, found again, child, childless, you, I . . . man turns and prays to God: "Lord, teach us to pray."

IV

DAYDREAMING OR LOVING?

As a word, meditation does strange things to people. It repels, it dries up, it produces many books. On the whole, it is a little awe-inspiring, marking a boundary between the life of a layman and the realm of priest, religious or pious retreat-maker. But it has no right to mark a boundary! Sometimes it is called mental prayer as a contrast to vocal prayer. This also puts it apart from the rush of the world. How very wrong if we allow its false appearance to deceive us. Meditation is open to all men.

It is important, first, to get a clear idea of the meaning in order to fathom the purpose. The dictionary probably has a definition if you will reach for it. Anyhow, for our prayer, meditation means taking some thought connected with God or the approach to God, and turning it over in our minds. That is only half the point, but it will do as a beginning. And so a good way to understand what we are aiming at in meditation is to follow the idea of the crossword puzzle. The clue to one across is "Who made you?" (Three letter word, first letter G). Such mind as a man has then starts to work out the possibilities. Already he is meditating. He is using his mind to develop some thought set in motion by the clue. The meditation is the solution of the puzzle based upon the key answer to one across. Every other clue radiates from there or returns there by a connection of idea or word. The interplay of these two, words and ideas, is interesting. Meditation may begin with either. Man can read first and so creep into prayer, or commence with vocal prayer, leading into mental prayer, or, again, the two may combine. In any case, the brain has somehow to be caught up in solving the crossword.

The part of the brain may be overemphasized. But man is called an intellectual animal, and the complete refusal of reason or imagination is therefore unnatural. Moreover, as these play an important rôle in man's activity, unless used to some extent, the mind will go whirling giddily away from God to frisk upon its own level. Used, the mind grows stronger by practice; it begins to grasp what the clues are getting at; it can glimpse the shape that the answer will outline. Facility increases. The previous insurmountable distractions, the drifting of the eye to gossip in the next column, sudden boredom, lack of concentration, all these evaporate in the joy of discovering that man is beginning to know God. The drudgery of going through the dictionary to get ideas gives place to the delight of meanings grasped when the clue is read. Perhaps the delight does not last, but for the moment do not worry about that. Keep on with the effort to learn more about God, not only from the books which give ideas to man, but from those ideas themselves which seed and germinate in man's own head.

Up till now, the whole emphasis has been upon the intellect. Man uses his power of imagination widely, so that meditation is often classed with a series of imaginative pictures, scenes from the Gospel and so on. These have their use. But it is a strictly limited and passing use, because however beautiful a picture we may conjure up, its attraction is not lasting as far as the mind is concerned and, even more important than that, we seek God and not an idea.

This introduces the second half of the point of the word meditation when used in reference to prayer. Always remember that this is no mere intellectual exercise, aided by the imagination. Meditation is a means of coming to prayer proper. Much of prayer, as has been stressed already, depends upon love. The burden of this is given in the Psalm, "I know no other content but clinging to God." The will, not the intellect, clings. In order to encourage the will to cling, the imagination is used to excite a movement of the will. This urging forward undertaken by the vividness of thought explains the purpose of meditating. The mind is useful in so far as it rouses the will. Abbot Chapman put it concisely when he wrote: "The object of meditation is to arrive at loving." How important this is! Unless the mind leads the will to make an act of love, man may simply daydream, centred upon himself, not reaching for God.

Take the first clue over again. The intellect ponders upon the answer and finds it is God. If the imagination is at all sensitive, it is struck by the immensity of this idea. God went to the trouble of making man. Man is nothing before God who is all. The more the mind dwells upon it, twists it, turns it, enlarges it and stands back to view it, the more impossible does it become to see satisfactorily the whole panorama. So the mind is forced to its knees, as it were, forced to adore the majesty, to praise the glory, to thank the goodness, to love God. It is the tale repeated of a man reaching a hilltop. With his eyes and mind he drinks in the landscape below, but can only express his wonder by a sigh. Thus prayer unites the nothingness of man to the all of God. Meditation has fulfilled its purpose. Meditation has arrived at loving.

A man following a book of meditations, following the Spiritual Exercises perhaps, is face to face with a cut and dried method of praying. It is a formula outwardly, which if applied will bring results. This can seem to some men completely alien to prayer. It is well, then, to know that progress for everyone usually passes through meditation. There is no absolute rule; this is the norm. Man goes wrong in his approach and application. He does not move forward with St Ignatius, who was very practical, seeing how the whole man must be employed. The teacher attracts his pupil towards incomprehensible words by use of pictures. These create an interest, but are not the end of the lesson, for they are teaching something further. Meditative pictures produce ideas; ideas foster resolutions. Take the mental or actual figure of Christ hanging on the Cross. How he suffers! That suffering is for me; more, I caused it; my reaction to the cause of suffering would be dislike; Christ's was love; his suffering brings salvation; it teaches me the value of suffering, of unselfishness; I suffer too, almost daily; can I use this? Lord, I will join with you in suffering! Thus endless ideas come into one channel from a single thought, and these in turn lead to a ceaseless possibility of expression: *Laudamus te. Benedicimus te. Adoramus te.*

But unless the build-up of thoughts brings the exclamation of love, it is wasted. Man's error is to get stuck in the picture, failing to find God. The mental picture soon fades, man tires trying to keep attention, and then says he cannot meditate. Nonsense! He does not know the way. He has started the engine, and not let in the clutch; he is stationary, getting nowhere. The mind-engine races or idles, until the clutch of the will to love is let in, till he presses forward to God; for the meditation is a means not an end.

Meditation in prayer-time therefore grows less as man advances towards God. Reading, walking, even working, his mind dwells somewhat on God, and as a result, when he comes to prayer proper, his will is keen to begin a loving act, without more preparation. For this, God must be our life-centre, and then, as Sister Elizabeth of the Trinity wrote, "Prayer is a rest, a relaxation. We come simply to him we love: we keep close to him, like a little child in its mother's arms, and let our hearts go out to him."

V

THOSE AWFUL DEVOTIONS

Sometimes the expression of a person's love is inexplicable to one who does not love. Because it is personal the way of expression may be useful to you and not to me, or *vice versa*. Thus rather aside from the general line of prayer as worked out in this series there lies the whole field of devotions and devotional practices within the Church. It may seem strange to give space to something which is seemingly obvious and of general benefit; but it would be false to ignore the place or value of devotions which are constantly recommended, though never enforced. At the same time, many are uncomfortable, if not unhappy, about the pious practices of the Church. Let us therefore consider the place of devotions.

Clearly, devotions are useful only in so far as they help souls towards God. Individuals and their prayer vary. The tendency to calculate holiness by the number of pious practices performed, the number of saints invoked, the number of medals, scapulars and Agnus Dei hung from the Rosary or person—this is beside the point. Burdensome prayer-quantities may stunt soul and body, an idea leading St Teresa of Avila to say, "From many devotions, Lord deliver us." Nevertheless, no individual has the right to condemn another's use of approved forms, even when repelled himself from such ways of praying. If laudable to the mind of the Church, yet unpalatable to some man, let him pray as best he can before God, allowing others the same freedom, together with sympathetic understanding. Intellectual snobbery does not go well with prayer. Man may reach heaven by

Plainsong or Palestrina, liturgy or rosary, by way of Carmelite, Franciscan, Dominican, Jesuit spirituality. His only obligation is to "pray always" by attending Mass and the Sacraments. Necessarily therefore what follows here scarcely touches the myriad devotions now practised, but may spotlight a few points.

THE BLESSED SACRAMENT

The centre of our spiritual life is the Blessed Sacrament, focused round our share in the Mass, fulfilled by frequent Communion. From this core have grown many devotions. Benediction, sometimes condemned by liturgically-minded people, is a simple and lovely method of acknowledging the Kingship of Christ ruling and blessing our lives. Holy Hour can become a regular monthly, weekly, even daily guard duty, mingling reparation and love. There is no surer way than this of basing our apostolate upon our Lord's appeal to "watch and pray". No conducted service is necessary; the Blessed Sacrament need not be exposed; it is enough to kneel or sit in His Majesty's presence. Hence the lesser, yet more necessary practice of visits to the Blessed Sacrament. Even if only for two minutes, everyone should pay such a visit daily, to talk to God or listen silently, regaining balance away from the teeming affairs of life; devotions may be used, but the old man knew the one necessary thing when he said, sitting wordless on a bench, "I looks at Him and He looks at me." That is the goal.

OUR LADY AND THE ROSARY

Outside the Church, criticism strikes at the Blessed Virgin as attracting idolatrous worship while side-tracking men from God. But the Church cannot substitute anyone for God. Later, in speaking of our Lady in the Liturgy, we shall see more fully that men are encouraged to love Mary because, as

Christ came to us through her, so we through her come to Christ. No other title is necessary but that of Mother of God; here lies all her glory, as is evident from the "Hail Mary". It is no wonder then that we urge our children continually to say "Hail Mary" in the rosary; at Lourdes, Fatima and elsewhere the appeal is the same; backed by the privileges showered upon it by many Popes, the rosary stands alone among devotions. Nevertheless, it is not necessary for salvation. Many, indeed, find it difficult to say, especially in public. In such difficulty, slow saying and meditating in private upon a decade or two, continued regularly for months, may lead subtly, without sense of development, to a love both for words and mysteries. No one should worry at inability over a long period; steady practice leads to further service and intercession of Mary. And do not think the rosary is for use only as a whole. Slipped into a pocket the fingers find it, the brain reacts to "Hail Mary" at odd moments of break or waiting during the day, the mind and heart rising to Jesus through Mary. If the junction of meditation and words distracts some, each must find the way best suited to him; undue effort on particular ideas may be fruitless; ring the changes of words and thoughts. Do not be discouraged at grasping neither; just keep on, lovingly. It should be added that the family rosary has received great support from Pope Pius XII; it is a meeting-ground for the apostolate of prayer in the family or friendly groups. Brevity may help; a single decade will suffice young children; trimmings can kill devotion.

THE STATIONS OF THE CROSS

Meditating on the Passion is the greatest way of understanding the effect of our sins. It deepens our love of Christ, shows us the place of sacrifice in redemption. From it should arise an intense desire to "fill up what is wanting in the sufferings of Christ". The Stations of the Cross fit this purpose. The public devotion may be distracting, painful, repugnant. Good! The way to Calvary was all these things. But there is no necessity to join a congregation. Prayers from a book can be omitted. To walk quietly from station to station in an empty church, halting longer here, passing quickly there, five minutes or half an hour, kneeling, standing, sitting—there are many Ways of the Cross. Some use this devotion in retreat or for Lent only. Yet the benefit would be great if more could spend ten minutes now and again round the stations. As with the rosary, initial dislike or difficulty can grow to love.

INDULGENCES AND THE HOLY SOULS

A word must be said about indulgenced prayers, because one object of the indulgence is to encourage devotion. All should appreciate the words of the convert's profession of faith on this subject, that "their use is most salutary to the Christian people". But do not be mere "indulgence hunters". Gladly accept what is given without feeling one prayer should yield to another which is more highly indulgenced, or that time is wasted in unindulgenced private prayer. By all means gain indulgences, never despise their use. A good method is two or three times a year to make a general intention to gain all indulgences accruing to every prayer during that period. These may be used personally or given to the Holy Souls, for to remember them is itself a particular devotion, very dear to every Catholic. There is no greater charity than to offer our suffering neighbours the result of our labours, to release them into heaven. Thus fulfilling Christ's work, many of the faithful themselves draw close to his Heart.

EXCLAMATIONS

The effort to Christianize ourselves, from rising, through Mass, work and free time and so to bed again, is aided by the

practice of frequent exclamations. They canalize our particular devotion to Christ, our Lady and so on. We may train ourselves to be God-conscious as we live the day, saying the
"Our Father" when shaving, "Come, Holy Ghost" when a
decision is asked, "My Lord and my God" when opening a
door, making the Sign of the Cross in temptation. The well-
known Jesuit, Father Willie Doyle, so far developed his
prayer life in this direction that he became accustomed to
saying literally hundreds of exclamations each hour, of love
of God, of offering, of contrition, of praise. Such a habit is
clearly helpful for anyone who is scatter-brained—and are we
not all?—for it brings God constantly before our minds, and
keeps his Holy Name holy upon our too easily profane tongues.
If anyone fears that this may become a mere habit and therefore disrespectful, I would say strongly that this was nonsense—an idle excuse to get away from a most spiritualizing
practice. Try it and see. I am confident the practice will
unite each to God, until the soul, schooled now to yearn for
God, cries with St Peter: "Lord, thou knowest that I love
thee."

VI

RECOLLECTION

SUPPOSE for a moment that what has gone before this chapter has merely been read and forgotten; suppose it has not entered your life. In that case, it has entirely missed the point. However much anyone has liked or disliked it, no progress has been made.

This might have happened owing to the pervading "not-for-me" attitude which jaundices so many minds in the approach to a more spiritual life. It is therefore necessary when considering the word "recollection" to stress it, not as something for the chosen few mystics, but as a basic necessity for all mankind—yes, you too! In particular, recollection is essential in the rush of modern city life, when man is escaping from himself and God in an endless round of noises, coloured lights, advertisements, electric timesavers, gadgets generally, all fixing thought on the narrow furrow of material things.

What then is recollection? It is the practice of a way of life, an attitude of mind, a disposition of heart, which leads us to turn back to God continually, wherever we are, whatever we are doing. It leads us from prayer and to prayer, permeating, saturating our existence with God-sense. Where your treasure is. . . .

Now, everyone has flashes of recollection, which go unrecognized for what they are; moments of stillness, when almost unperceived, we are experiencing the close presence of God; man alone on a hilltop; man sniffing the air after a thunderstorm; man on a ship at sea. These are natural to all, but they grow or decline according to our preparation for

36

them in the life we lead. Thus, the object of silence, routine, penance in a contemplative order is to allow body, mind, and soul to cultivate the realization of the *kingdom of God within you*, an awareness spreading through the soul so that it sees God in others; spreading also to the things of nature which show forth God's glory; spreading through the actions and reactions which make up life, lighting up the finger of Providence guiding each chance happening towards our salvation. St. Catherine of Genoa, for instance, quietly concentrated each moment upon God's special gift of joy, suffering, effort, decision; a method praised by the Jesuit writer de Caussade as "the sacrament of the present moment".

This is important. An average man or woman has very little obvious opportunity for prolonged prayer during the day. And yet there is no alteration to the Scriptural command, *pray without ceasing*. Prayer therefore must be adapted to the situation, not crushed out altogether. The leakage proves how it is crushed. We know it from our own experience of slipping away from the prayer-time.

Recognize the problem! Distractions in life lead to distraction in prayer. Face the problem! It is happening to ourselves now. The remedy is to attempt to realize more often that we are living in the presence of God. That is possible by living in the present moment, neither worried for the future or glamourizing the past. It requires practice. Man is bound to be swept again into cares; he forgets that God cares; he forgets that the present indigestion, the probable bad weather, ever-present financial troubles are all recognized and allowed by God. It requires humility and strong action to grasp this, because we do too much in self-reliance. Driving on independently, we break down for lack of spiritual power. The troubles, joys or hard work that God allows will not harm us, provided we are centred upon him, acknowledging that all things come from him, a collar stud or the loss of a collar stud, every breath a gift and so a praise of his glory. Recollection is simply a recognition again and again of this truth.

Now, to acquire the habit of referring all things to God, it is essential to review the use of time during the day. Many claim it is so crowded that no moment is left for prayer; frequently people are "too busy to go to Mass". That is akin to heresy; it is madness. Yet many firmly believe it to be a fact. Supposing I demanded on pain of losing your soul, that you should set aside one hour a day for reflection, seeing no one, listening to no radio, watching no television, not even reading a book or paper, would you not say I was crazy, that I failed to understand modern difficulties? Just because I understand, I demand, if not an hour, at very least a quarter of an hour, alone, unhurried, silent before God. This must become a habit in your life. It is essential to a spirit of recollection; it is basic to prayer; it is urgent with the urgency of life or death; because the preparation for prayer is made in the time before, outside prayer. Only by stopping short, entering into ourselves, ruminating, getting the situation into perspective, can we balance the insignificance of the material against the infinite simplicity of God. Dashing from the office desk via a quick telephone call, to attempted prayer means dashing into distractions; the mind is still dialling! Try instead to go quietly, sitting silent in front of God, then you will take God back with you to the desk.

Is this out of the question? No! We allow ourselves to become harried by the world. How unnecessary, for the world will pass away! St Vincent de Paul said, "Give me a man of prayer, and he will be capable of doing anything." We can grow into men of prayer, enclosing each action in a cocoon of prayer; continual acts are impossible, but we can learn to live in a state of prayer. That high-sounding phrase is not beyond any man. It implies the effort to centre our lives on God. Prayer is not just the short time on our knees, it must come and go between and in work and play, as the sun appears and disappears between the clouds. The presence of God, like the sun, is there, even when covered by a cloud of worldly affairs; subconsciously we are still aware of the divine sun shining behind our darkness, in the depth of the soul. Yet true union with God only develops amid a certain stillness and silence. Life without these is empty of any deep love of God, missing the very point of living. It is also using too much human energy to achieve so little. Economically, it is wise to abandon some time to God in meditation and recollection; you will be repaid a hundredfold, *growing in wisdom and grace before God and man*. For it is easy to tell when you are in the company of a recollected man; it is manifest in his serenity.

Each soul has the duty, and it is a stiff one, of filling his immediate circle with something of the atmosphere which pervades the enclosure of a contemplative order. No soul will do this unrecollected. No soul will do this, if he waits for silence to come. He must make silence round himself, in the midst of hubbub if necessary. To do so, he must school himself to certain fixed silences, withdrawals from the world, mentally and even physically, daily retreats into the interior of his own soul. This action will increase realization of God's presence at other less peaceful periods. He will be able to turn more readily to spiritual refreshment. Finally, he will find it possible to follow the advice of Archbishop Goodier to a person living in the world: "You should try, without any painful effort, to dwell upon God as often as longing for recollection, and regret that you cannot cultivate it more, comes upon you. It will not do to wait for disengaged moments when you can close your door and be alone. The moment in which we crave after recollection is the moment in which to practise it. Turn your heart then and there to God, simply, familiarly, trustfully."

VII

SIMPLE STEPS TOWARDS MENTAL PRAYER

Now—I am going to say all over again the things I said in the previous chapters!

No, it is not quite so bad as you may think. Sometimes it happens that the same thing said in a different way, with a slightly different emphasis perhaps, may manage to work a revolution, where before it merely rolled from the duck's back. You see, we must keep on trying.

St Francis de Sales said, "Stand on tiptoe and you will reach heaven." We are attempting to raise our minds and hearts as though, on tiptoe, we reach for the top of a wall, to lever ourselves up for a view of the promised land. We cannot see over; we can only occasionally grip the top of the wall with our fingers. We stretch up—there, we had a glimpse over for a moment. Now, it is gone again.

We were fools to think we could climb up. We were fools even to try; better give up at once, before we overbalance and strain ourselves . . . or shall we make one more effort?

Yes, keep trying, keep trying. Do not give up yet.

Most of our prayer life is dreadfully humdrum. Everyone wants to give up. But then, the majority of us, admit it or not, are humdrum too.

The revolution is to turn the humdrum into the holy. You do this by prayer and more prayer; by love and more love; then there is a point in living in the humdrum.

The general lethargy and even fear of the spiritual is often a vague idea that to advance in prayer is to take on a task which is going to demand too high a price from all who

SIMPLE STEPS TOWARDS MENTAL PRAYER   41

persevere. It is easier and safer, we think, not to delve deeply into these matters; they are not for us; with Francis Thompson we see the attraction, and each echo:

> *Yet was I sore adread*
> *Lest having Him, I must have naught beside.*[1]

What nonsense! How we deceive ourselves. We do not see that He is ALL.

So, remaining quite ordinary in our daily humdrum round, when, where, and how do we pray? The first two queries need occupy little time, for we take the Gospel very literally here. We must begin now and pray always. There is no exaggeration; there is not even a "but", and, therefore, please do not put one in. Face up to it, now and always. And that rather answers the "where" as well as the "when", especially if we recall the dictum of that early spiritually-minded man— Cassian, was it not?—who maintained: "He prays but little and but badly, who only prays when on his knees." There are differences of method, degree, and situation, but the "always and everywhere" remains unchanged.

How to pray? Do not laugh at or ignore the truism—the only way to learn to pray is to pray. This hard plain fact is skated over by some. Do not forget, either, that we shall not be praying properly until we do not know that we are praying. Both these phrases must be considered, and then practised. Be quite sure of this, prayer we shall not learn from books or people; we shall only come to know from hours of dull, knee-aching waste-of-time prayer, alone by ourselves. Books may help; the experience of others may encourage; advice may clear the air; but fro: - the beginning to the end it is the actual getting down to pray by the individual which is the only real schooling. Then, under the grace of God, it is the being faithful through stone walls, over precipices, in dry

[1] *The Hound of Heaven*

darkness; it is trust in emptiness, love in desolation, peace in suffering. Above all it is humility in failure, for God's economy is based on failure, so that only by failing in prayer shall we succeed.

If we are thoroughly law-abiding (good citizens, that is), we go into the House of God by the main door of prayer. On doing so, we may be inclined to think that there is not very much of interest on the ground floor. The chief utensil displayed is labelled "vocal prayer", and though most of us glance at it in a half-hearted way, the more eager are looking for better gifts, while the lazy are too idle to try their hand even at this, particularly when they find that there is quite a lot of drudgery and repetition required. Nevertheless, there is nothing more important than beginning correctly and learning the hard way, though it may seem tiresome. Now, when the apostles saw the attractiveness of our Lord's prayer-time, they asked him to teach them to pray. He did so; and the instructions they left behind for us to follow were: "Say: 'Our Father' . . ." It is important to stress this, as vocal prayer can be despised by good people, probably because it is misunderstood. We all, normally, begin at some time: "God bless Mummie and Daddie." Very soon we are saying, "God bless me, and Mummie and Daddie—Oh! And don't forget Bingo, my teddy bear," which, if you come to look at it, is already a tendency towards prayer which is more than vocal. We are starting to bring our minds into it, to think; and this is natural, even from the Catechism definition. But thinking is the embryo of definition.

Surely, then, this will be a comfort to those who imagine that they are stuck at vocal prayer, who fear the term "mental prayer", who cannot get beyond what might be called "Garden of the Soul spirituality", that is, set vocal prayers, recited or read from a book. It is necessary to understand that even here on the ground floor mental prayer begins, for vocal prayer implies a degree of mental prayer. Though I am not suggesting that the two are the same, this idea of one growing upon the other can be dwelt upon by those especially who live in the world. The mind is normally engaged on outside, mundane thoughts and cares; some use of vocal prayer curbs "the restless little butterfly of the mind", giving it a tangible reality to supply the place of the worldly tangibles which otherwise crowd in upon our prayers. What is more, if we keep ahead through this ground floor, we find that in the centre it develops into a lift, open to *all* and carrying us up to *all* the other floors in God's House of Prayer. Thus we can quite safely say that no one ever entirely puts aside vocal prayer as finished for him or her in this life. And the best examples we can give of this fact are the last prayer of our Lord, "Father, into thy hands", and such glories as the *Magnificat* of our Lady, or even the Canticle of the Sun from St Francis of Assisi.

But note this carefully: if vocal prayer forms a lift, we can get into it or refuse to get into it; having got in, we can, as it were, refuse to push the button, so that the lift never works. Or, having gone up, we can refuse to get out at the next floor, but push the button and come down again. For the general teaching is that the stage after vocal prayer is meditation, and we can refuse any great degree of this exercise, if we wish. It is a development of vocal prayer, but comes into a new category. Given a glass of wine, we can gulp it down, holding our noses, or sip it, enjoying the tasting. So, we can gabble through the "Our Father", or, like St Teresa, get stuck at the beauty and meaning of the first words, turning them over in our minds again and again.

There is nothing very difficult in it. There is nothing very rigid. If one person is helped by dividing the Passion into sections, making points and resolutions, well and good. Another will prefer to read a passage from the Gospel and

sit digesting it. A third may be wrapped up in the consideration of the humility of our Lady, or the mercy of Jesus to
Mary Magdalen, or the glory of the Resurrection. If a person
can draw something from any of these, by any method, or by
no method, he is not wasting his time, or God's. Provided one
thing! Prayer is not a theological exercise, nor is it a scriptural
study. Recall again the often quoted words of Dom John
Chapman, "The object of meditation is to arrive at loving."
So long as thinking about these passages of the Gospel, these
virtues of our Lady, so long as that kindles a spark of love in
our hearts and leads to an act of love, that long is it useful.
After that, we must pass on to something else, another consideration if it helps, or just to continue simply loving. There
may be a day when everything makes us love; another when
our toes are cold, our heads ache, we are liverish, and the
water was not hot . . . then we must just sit or kneel, giving
God our restless pain. We have vocal prayer to fall back on;
we have the Rosary, where meditation spreads out inde-
finitely, or can be cut down to the merest glance at God.
Some can say the Rosary at all times, others are never at ease
with it; this one likes doing the Stations, another cannot bear
them; another dips into the Gospel for balm.

Here we have "the freedom of the children of God", because we should approach God in our own way and not in
someone else's. There are a few, very few, fairly safe rules, like
the fact that most people must go through a stage of meditation, which may last a long or short time. But beyond that, the
method is an individual and simple approach to God by use
of mind and heart, most particularly of heart, since this is
certainly true . . . love is the means of our union with God
in this world. It is quite natural, then, as in human friendship,
that there should be a growth; it is unnatural to say that such
a growth is not meant for us, for dwarfs are freaks. And, of
course, if we are growing, we may also grow out of our

method, as a plant which is too big has to be repotted; left to twine its roots inside, it will never flourish; given room, it will expand. But repotting needs courage.

Before considering that, one other thought. Meditation may be all right when we are getting down to a fixed period laid aside for prayer. What about the rest of the day—nine-tenths, very often? When we try to pray, all these hours come crowding in. What about that?

Quite simple: prayer-time must push out into the world to prevent the world pushing into prayer-time, because attack is the best form of defence. Logically, then, the day must be planned to fit prayer-time, not *vice versa*. It is a big reversal of our normal policy, but it can be done. And from that point, we can take our prayer with us always, learning to be re-collected and to live in the presence of God. To start and to continue, no method is too childish; a man carrying his rosary loose in his pocket can say it on the bus or train, in the street, in the cinema or fish queue—sanctifying himself and the unthinking crowds around him. Another may prefer to make an ejaculation each time he opens a door, goes up-stairs, or puts a full stop on the typewriter. In factories I know, some bless the name of Jesus each time it is taken in vain around them, turning even sin to sanctity.

It is in this way that we canalize our thoughts to God, spreading peace and prayer through all our lives, as we take God to places where he is most neglected. For this purpose, nothing is more simple or sure than the rosary, ready to hand in a pocket, where the fingers may slip automatically to the beads as soon as they have no other job to do, be it when we are strap-hanging in a crowded Underground, or sitting waiting for the kick-off.

But this is vocal prayer again—not mental? You miss the point! These are only little methods, outside the fixed times of prayer, helping us to build up what must become a general

atmosphere of God-love in our life. To help this background
it is wise each day to read for a short while from one spiritual
book which appeals to us, thus gaining food for meditation;
perhaps, also, if possible, we can lay aside ten minutes in
which to sit, relaxed, quiet, alone, in God's presence. Many
will say at once that such action in a busy life means instant
drowsiness and no prayer. I will only quote Péguy as an
answer:

> *But I tell you, says God, that I know of nothing so beautiful in the
> whole world*
> *As a little child going to sleep while he is saying his prayers*
> *Under the wing of his guardian angel*
> *And laughs happily as he watches the angels and begins to go to sleep;*
> *And is already mixing his prayers together and no longer knows
> what they are all about;*
> *And sticks the words of Our Father among the words of Hail Mary,
> all in a jumble. . . .*[1]

How often our prayer may be a mere battle of the eyelids (it
was with St Teresa of Lisieux). Do not worry about that, and
above all, do not give up your prayer-time for that reason.

But supposing we remain faithful to prayerful meditation
and try to be recollected during the day, living a generally
good life, seeking God with a single mind . . . then at some
time or other our prayer will be modified, because the meditations, the thinking parts, gradually get less, while the acts,
the loving parts, grow. We find a series of forced acts are the
main portion of our prayer, and this is often hard.

We have somewhere in this period to take our courage in
both hands and get out of the lift at the next floor. It is difficult; it needs courage; it may have to be done unaided, even
hindered. For the lift attendant, who is the spiritual director,
is often keener to come down to the lower floor, where he
personally feels more secure. Do not be misled. Be absolutely

---

[1] *Innocence and Experience*, tr. by Julian Green (Pantheon Books Inc.)

sure that God asks from you generosity and love; he will do the rest.

What, then, is the difficulty? Simply this: that only when the lift has left us do we realize that we are being stranded on a floor which has no floor. We have the awful sensation of stepping out into mid-air. In other words, our tangible feelings, the mental pictures of meditation—all these are gone. We are left clutching frantically at any familiar object, unable to understand. We are lost; surely we have gone wrong? We try meditating, and it doesn't work. We try the Rosary and the Stations; they just dry us up. What then? Will a dose of salts do any good? It might; it is worth trying. But if not?

Suppose that we are really trying to love God, that we desire him "in spirit and in truth", that we can get nothing from meditation, that we meet dryness wherever we turn . . . that we are, in fact, on tiptoe reaching over the wall-top and cannot grasp our object—God. Suppose all this—then the signal light is certainly at "Go".

Yes, go ahead, happy souls, in darkness unseeing, in dryness unfeeling, in loneliness unknowing. This is indeed the time for courage and perseverance, which the rich days of meditation and joy have been fertilizing, because now is the time for the seed of prayer, being sown in good ground, to die that it may yield fruit; the Word must go that the Spirit may come, to "teach you all things".

Many of us will want to turn back, many good men will encourage us to do so, but we must go on just the same, confidently surrendering, willing to drop into space on the faith that God's love intangibly supports us, Now and again our finger-tips touch heaven: most of the time, the wall is very tall, very dark, nakedly unyielding. But all the same, the deep knowledge is there that all things are worth while, if we but keep on tiptoe, until God gives us the spiritual stature sufficient to unite us to himself.

VIII

GENEROSITY IN PRAYER

You are called to be saints! It is perfectly clear that anyone can grasp the meaning of that sentence; but a meaning grasped does not necessarily produce a reaction. When I began I said my object was to point out that the immediate call to prayer is personal and individual, with no exception for age or occupation. It applies to each person because each person has a soul. Therefore it applies to you, and failure to understand will place you in the position of the Scotsman who, arriving at the gates of heaven and amazed to find what he should have done in life, exclaimed to St Peter, "I didna ken"; to which the key-bearer replied, "Ye ken noo." No excuse is plausable before the living God at the judgement, hence an ostrich-life now is a bad investment. We must be realistic. The first real fact is the hardest. This business of becoming a saint. Quite impractical, contrary to daily bread and income-tax. It is for most people the mixing of drinks and devotions, aligning Trade Unions with mysticism, praying on the merry-go-round, meditating on the Underground. Fantastic! But real with a stone-cold-sober reality of commandment—pray always.

Hard work! Ah, now we are at the basic reality! Yes, it is hard work, almost heroic work. For that reason it demands an enormous generosity or willingness. Chesterton, in *The Man who was Thursday*, pictured Syme, the new recruit to the movement, as interviewed by Sunday in a darkened room. Accepted, Syme tries to back out saying he has no qualifications. Sunday replies that willingness alone is necessary. Syme

48

has heard of no profession with only willingness as the test of membership. "I have," says Sunday; "Martyrs. I'm condemning you to death. Good afternoon."

There you are! That is what God asks—complete willingness to undertake his work in this world, a veritable martyrdom of human will and desire. There is a choice. That is our danger. The rich young man went so far, but could not bring himself to real generosity; he was, one might say, willing to join Catholic Action passively. Mary Magdalen was repentant, utterly willing to give herself and her possessions, no matter what a fool she looked, what a cost it meant. Here we may place our home-made barrier! Continually, we thwart the work of God because we are unwilling to accept the price which active co-operation demands. It is hard, indeed, to give up time honour, gaiety, in this world.

Note this. It may be harder for the professional, the more highly educated person. He may have too many interests, too many ties; his position and his cares may be incompatible with the service of God. Did not Christ say it was harder for the rich man . . .? What a charge this can be! It is harder, therefore it needs more generosity. But does that generosity exist realistically? In some cases, yes. In far the greater majority sadly, but definitely, it does not.

Let us acknowledge the fact that to convert England and the world we need a hundred per cent more generosity of our time, of our self, of our whole outlook. The spirit of crusade must burn in us; there must be determination to bring Christ the King back to reign in men's hearts. And this must place all our personal considerations second to the one thing necessary.

As it is, everything is always hedged with qualifications. Theoretically we accept Catholic Action; we even complain that no action is being undertaken. Yet when it comes to doing something concrete there is an excellent reason why we personally cannot be involved. Weekday Mass individually or as a group? What about you? Not every day! And you— you'd rather not promise? And you cannot guarantee. Well then a Rosary or a visit? You would rather not be pinned down: it is too like regimentation: you dislike working by numbers!

Of course! But unless there is some standard, some corporate acts, some discipline which makes us exert ourselves, even inconveniences us, we are not making much sacrificial effort. We have grown up in unreality, confess it or not. Self-interest obscures the perspective, blurring the initiative and drive necessary for God's work through lay people. Hide-bound by conventional ideas of what constitutes a spiritual and truly Catholic life, self ousts God. The depth of our spiritual forces compares badly with the thrust of the Communist mystique. We degenerate to discussion, endless and empty, because the tremendous possibility envisaged in theory is not fattened upon generous gift in prayer: *Parturiunt montes et nascetur ridiculus mus.*

We are totally inadequate for the part we need to play. Drive off complacency. Every effort, possible and seemingly mad, must be made to allow God to found in us that hard core of spirituality without which the apostolate is so much self-centred idealism. It is useless to imagine that anyone can be a Catholic, a member of Christ, and not suffer intensely in this life, suffer inconvenience, dislocation. We should be nagged all the time by the necessity of prayer and penance in the growth of the mystical body. Active participation, guaranteed at Confirmation, should re-orientate our life. Demands should grow, and with this, love and desire grow too.

The more man gives the more there is to give. Give nothing and you may be sure you will feel satisfied that you are giving sufficient! Today it is totally unreasonable to expect life to be turned upside down for religion? It is expected nevertheless. In no other way will action become action, out of a labyrinth of words. Faith, humility, obedience, prayer—these demand high generosity from modern man.

Make no mistake. The foundation of every apostle is daily Mass and Communion. How presumptuous to imagine we can build the Body without sharing the sacrifice of the Head. Far better for a man to go to Mass daily than to belong to an organization. Not all can go every day. But how very many could, if they were not blinded by "impossible" inconveniences. From the Mass will flow action. Alas, action does not always lead to more frequent Mass. Too easy is the excuse of late nights and early office hours. A hard saying, but less hard than the Cross.

Let every would-be apostle, no! every Catholic person, ask the question: Am I only a pretender? "I say, therefore, it is by their fruits that you will know them. The kingdom of heaven will not give entrance to every man who calls me Master, Master: only to the man that does the will of my father who is in heaven." And against that put St Paul: "His will, your sanctification." Is it too much to expect that Christ shall have an answer when he stands as king lifting his voice and saying: "If any man will come after me, let him deny himself and take up his cross daily and follow me"? Not once a week—daily. Face it! Courage! Through prayer, spiritual reading, and the generosity necessary to produce time and willingness, go ahead towards the flowering of unity and union.

The way goes ahead, through darkness and unutterable barrenness to unutterable joy. There is no barrier across the road unless we refuse the toll of generosity. Each step is for all of us, but each step is in obscurity against commonsense and natural feelings. The road mounts a rugged hillside shrouded in cloud. Below in the valley all that we might do, comfort, easy triumphs, human love beckon from lush green fields, dimpled with sunlight, along the other route. On the mountain, even our friends proclaim our intentions nonsense. Yet the only demand is that the traveller press on, losing with each step something that man holds dear. And always up there ahead is a shadow across the path, a shadow with outstretched arms, hanging from a cross. Often it is too dark to distinguish properly, but ever and again it seems a voice says: "Come," while those pierced hands are somehow beckoning.

IX

INTERLUDE

Now then!

Have *you* made any new effort to build your life on a fuller, firmer basis of prayer?

It is simply no good finding any reason in the world for not doing so, for I can tell you now that your reason will be false, even if it seems true in worldly terms. Whatever your life is, it begins and should therefore end in Life, in God. It can only make sense more fully in so far as it is ordered to God through prayer.

You say that is all very well for me to write, but. . . .

Oh dear! How God must dislike that little word "but". It will get you out of anything unpleasant in this world. I grant you that. It will never get you out of hell in the next.

I know what I am saying is hard. That is the reason I am saying it. I know it would be nice to say "but it does not apply to me". Unfortunately, or fortunately, it does apply to you and me. It is hard as the wood of the Cross was hard. It is difficult as the way of the Cross was difficult.

Yet, the way is not altogether lonely. God has provided in the Church a guide and a companion. Through each year this wonderful society which he has built reminds us individuals that we are also a body, the Mystical Body. She makes us live not only with our life, but with the life of the Church, the life of Christ. That is why she gives us the continual example of the saints in her calendar, the repetition each year of the joys, sorrows and glory of God made Man.

Take courage from seeing the way others have gone

before you. Take new hope from the liturgy. Take and give love as you go through the Scriptures, seeing every season, every feast of our Lord, our Lady or the saints as new nourishment overflowing upon the thirsty soul.

Though you long to go back to the easy days before you began to pray, do not do so. There is everything to lose if you do. Anyone can go back. But God is calling you on.

There are a hundred thousand excuses. Scrap them all. Plunge instead into the prayer-life of the Church.

God is calling you on and on and on. Your own prayer-life will grow too as knowledge grows in growing love. Press on!

II

LIVING THROUGH THE LITURGY

X

EXPECTATION—THE MAN

CHRISTIANITY is a life. The Church helps the penetration of all life with the doctrine of Christ. But, far from the notion of those who scoff at her, she insists that her children are active in their understanding of their faith. She sets out to teach by every possible method. She develops the prayer-life of the people through gestures and actions as well as through the common notion of prayer.

The problem that faces us now is to glimpse a light here and a shadow there in the liturgical calendar of the Church, which will aid us to use the feasts and fasts better than before.

Because it is a whole life, therefore every aspect of life is covered. We can only look at parts, but we must keep one point clearly before our minds as they grow in faith.

The Mass is the centre, the hub from which all the rest of life radiates in this world of grace and nature. That is why each feast is celebrated by a special Mass. The particular lesson of the day or season is brought out through the Mass.

If we grow in faith, we must learn to grow in humility, taking as a watchword St John the Baptist's phrase, "He must increase but I must decrease." In the Catechism, prayer comes under the section of hope. Now, hope looks forward, based upon faith, trusting God's promise.

Hope today is an empty word. We live always in expectancy, an expectancy which is increased by a continual spiral of crises, spiritual, temporal, domestic or international. These in turn make us think of our era as outstanding in history, singular in development or disaster. But that should emphasize more than anything else the continual paradox of the Gospel, where we are told to die in order to live. It should also encourage us to realize that the problems remain much the same in each generation, in fact that our lives are an overlap, as it were, of time and eternity. The two mingle almost inextricably until sometimes we are not sure of time, past, present or to come. Now and again, we seem to have dived back to childhood; at another period, we are suspended away from time, only fearing the moment when we must be plunged back into the turmoil of clocks, timetables, dates.

St Augustine hailed God as "ever old and ever new"; in one sense, the world is as old as time, in another it is shiningly new, because the hands of God's clock point always to the beginning. "Before Abraham was, I am." God speaks thus. But as for creatures, they are old and new in time, yet all equal in God's eternity, so that here and now we sit stilly present with Abraham, Isaac and Jacob, with David and Jonathan, with Jeremias and the Machabees, with John the Baptist, with Christ. What a terrifying reality of timelessness! We cannot grasp it, we seldom dare to face it, because it throws into such violent contrast our petty worries about the next few days—none of which matter, for God's Providence covers all.

Each year, Advent brings out something of this time and timeless paradox, the growth of new from old, the insufficiency of man before God. Coming as it does at the ending of a secular year, Advent brings in for the Church a new year. Already before mankind is finished discarding the old, God has proclaimed the new. So always through the history of his creation has God anticipated the needs of his creatures, always fulfilling, never destroying. Eve falls, and at once the second Eve is foreshadowed crushing the serpent's head; man is driven from paradise, and as he goes, God announces a return to paradise through redemption; the sun of Saul sets, and the star of David rises. Man standing to gaze at the stars in a darkened world, wonders momentarily at the majesty of it all, so far beyond his grasp . . . he wonders, and then goes in to divert his mind with less difficult considerations.

Man is, as it were, midway between God and his material creation—part of him reaching up to the stars, part leaning earthily to earth. Man thus holds a position of great pride, where he has every reason for humility.

From the beginning, everything was made to give glory to God. God cannot make a thing which will not give him glory. And man's part most particularly was to glorify, because man was most perfect. Therefore the depth of his fall cannot now be measured by that human mind which was once so pure that it could see God. We can only calculate the ages between Adam and John the Baptist to glimpse the slowness with which that re-perfecting was accomplished. And even so, this was a limited rehabilitation, a perfecting in expectation, by which the people were taught to look for their saviour, the son of man, somehow mysteriously connected with Yahwe, the One God, whose Trinity was still unknown. Each woman in this time might bear the saviour; each first-born male might be the saviour.

The prophets, anointed heralds of the saviour, looked forward to his coming. So too the priests, the anointed servants, and the kings, the anointed regents, each stood individually as the type of him who was to come. And not only these important persons, but each single human being in creation built up in a tiny, God-planned way the perfection of mankind until "the earth be opened and bud forth a saviour".

When it began to happen, it all happened quite suddenly, quite silently; it happened to a man and woman. The woman was Elizabeth, and we see her carrying out God's method of confounding the wisdom of men, regardless of time. She was old, the story tells us, past the years for bearing children, yet longing and confident still that a child would be entrusted to her. How she differed from some modern women!

So she lived on, coming gradually to hope more and more against hope. Not a very exciting life, surrounded by a small circle so that when she did at last conceive, "she hid herself five months." You can almost hear the gossip starting; you can feel the sneers of the neighbours rising up against this ageing couple for having a child at all at their time of life. This is the sort of way in which God treats his chosen, with humiliation to temper his gifts against our human pride, as we must all come quickly to understand. Then her son is born, and the father, Zachary, is allowed to be a dumb and useless laughing-stock, who cannot even name his heir. The people, those who are always quick to know what is right, jostle each other in their haste to lay down the law, saying the name is not John—but John it has to be, for the old man laboriously writes the name to end their loud objections—the law of man must bend before the law of God.

At once Zachary and Elizabeth fade from the scene, like so many of God's saints, and leave behind the gaunt shadowy figure of John, who is so timeless and so typical that people cannot place him: "Art thou Elias?" and he answered no, "or a prophet or the saviour?" We are not told much of his early life, indeed he seems hardly to have had one; perhaps his two parents did not long survive his birth. For otherwise it would seem strange that at an early age he retires into the desert and there is no indication that the secret knowledge Elizabeth had of Mary's child was passed on to John, her son.

This is one of those strange, uneconomical incidents which seem so untidy to man's mind and are so much the pattern of God's plan. It is difficult to remember that John was only a few months older than Jesus. So often, in imagination, the preaching of the Baptist could have preceded the birth of

Christ, as the Church today places it in Advent. Whereas in reality, it did not happen long before Christ too began his public ministry. Here again, time and the timeless telescope —the lesson is still the same, the way has still to be prepared. Side by side, yet far apart, John and Jesus grow before God, so that when we read of John during Advent, it is quite a different advent which he is heralding, the advent of Christ the man, not Christ the child, which we await before each Christmas.

Yet John is the typical figure of expectancy, because you could almost say that he was announcing one to come who was already there; that John's "the kingdom of God is at hand" is echoed at once by Christ as "the kingdom of God is within you", that John was conscious of his mission, yet unconscious of the whereabouts of the one he was announcing. Art shows us John and Jesus playing at their mothers' knees, the Gospel hints rather at John's separation and lack of exact knowledge, until he suddenly lifts his eyes and is inspired to say "Behold the lamb of God".

This is just the difference between the way man would arrange a publicity campaign, and the way God allows us to work out our lives just in naked faith—crying in the wilderness. For it is not really the results which God seeks, but the utter willingness to give, the complete attempt not to count the cost. And this he found in John the Baptist.

No enviable rôle was given to this last of the prophets. Perhaps more than any other, the prophet has to teach by his example how all men must live by faith, a hard, cold, dark, all-enveloping faith. To judge his early schooling, you would have to read deeply into the Old Testament, weighing the dumbness of Ezechiel, the tears of Jeremias, the flight of Jonas. Like all the prophets, he was quite insufficient in himself, and served God's purpose simply because he was carried away by the Spirit, a man emptied of himself, and so much the more possessed of God. His training was in the desert, which is no paradise of technicolor films, his diet was locusts and honey, not so delicate a fare as they might sound from a distance. And just because of all this, John stands out for us as a lasting example of the spiritual life.

He was doing penance, driven on by Faith. Faith was his guiding star, and the more anyone advances by way of faith, the darker the night becomes. So with John, the more awe-inspiring and fascinating his message was for people as it became clearer through the way he lived it. The more it drove him to the wilderness, away from the stream of life, the more he was sought by the world, just as today we find streams of motor coaches queueing to enter the grounds of enclosed monasteries. John became as much as anything a spectacle, which somehow produced magnetic power, which gathered disciples, even though what he said was so far from man's pleasure.

To many, he was foreshadowing the words of St Paul, being "a fool for Christ's sake", but here was even greater foolishness, because St Paul had seen the fulfilment, John had not. John was completely Christocentric in his preaching —but he preached in expectation of what was to happen; he had no backing from the Jews; there was no Church and no sacramental system to uphold what he said. John worked with signs as Ezechiel had done, but he baptized only with water. John imposed severe penance upon himself and his disciples, for a future reward, and had to bear the seeming contradiction when Christ came.

We do not hear of John working miracles as he preached, for he was preaching faith, and to see is not to believe. So he preached truth in and out of season, he preached against the habits of the people, he preached against the illicit marriage of Herod the tetrarch, just as we might have to do today. He was hardly a popular figure. What prophet ever was? But he was a power in the land. Truth had to be maintained; he knew that he alone could not do it, as he was insufficient; but he knew he must still preach the truth even it if meant the loss of his head. Looked at cold-bloodedly in the light of faith, the loss of the head is nothing to man beside the loss of truth. This is the truth of the martyr, to whom the cry of eternity makes a louder clamour than the alarm of time.

Here we strike the deep meaning of John the Baptist. It is a lesson still valid today for us, since we too are awaiting God, and we too in our own sphere have to be heralds of the truth. A herald is only there to hold the stage for a moment. His very being as a herald demands that he steps aside for all to see the one he heralds. "He must increase, but I must decrease." John's motto applies to each one of us, for whether we precede or follow Christ in time, God is timeless, and we are only his heralds.

So often in life, the burden of our office, the pride of place, the fine figure we are cutting, these obscure the truth that we are only ambassadors; taken up with self-indulgence, with self-preservation, or just with self, we forget we are not the central point upon which all human existence depends. We cannot look at John and feel comfortable about our pride and self-sufficiency, those two complementary vices which bring England to its knees today. St Ignatius it was who pointed always to the longest and last battle, the battle against self. Each one of us, to a greater or lesser degree, builds this soft cocoon of self, light, almost beautiful in texture, yet sufficient to destroy our complete surrender to God.

It is the object of entering a contemplative order to fulfil the motto of John. But it is not only for contemplatives that John spoke. He spoke for us all, in or out of the world. He demanded that we should grow less full of self-confidence, while trusting more in God. To do this asks of us a great faith. Faith in its turn takes us beyond the bounds of human understanding to what our neighbours regard as stupidity or even madness, but which may be better described as truth flowering in humility. This is why John is the voice crying in the wilderness—crying that is against so much of worldly wisdom however ancient or modern it may be.

John stood in expectancy, pointing. He pointed to a revolution in life by his life; he pointed to the kingdom of God, which was already come among men; he pointed to the loss of life as the means of gaining new life.

Because men looked to him for a message, he became a signpost. Like all true signposts, he carried a message; yet the message did not point to himself, but on beyond himself. His message was "Behold the Lamb of God". Like the signpost, his object was to point. The traveller goes beyond the signpost and, if he perseveres, he finds the city to which it is pointing. Then the signpost may be forgotten. It is the city which is important.

In the case of John and his pointing, the city was doubly important to the traveller, because it was the City of God.

That was the story of the Baptist.

He showed his deep humility in understanding the secondary rôle man always plays in the work of God. Unlike the temporal leader, the man of God is to be a signpost, pointing men on to the one who comes after but "is preferred before me". His difficulty, humanly speaking, was in being humble enough to go on pointing in fulfilment of the law, even when he had already been superseded by Christ. And the final demand from his humility was, after a life of expectancy, to die still expectant, before the redemption which he had foretold.

He showed complete faith in abandoning himself to a life of madness in the worldly sense, fearlessly contradicting wrongdoers, high and low. His faith was complete, because a prophet's gift is for the use of others, not for the comfort

of his own soul. It was complete too, because he continued
to point even when darkness swept over his soul. We can see
in his disciples' question when he sent them saying, "Art
thou the Christ?", not only a pointer to strengthen their
faith, but a plea for reassurance, to lighten the all-pervading
gloom of prison, when everything had come to naught and his
message had been disregarded.

His message continues to be disregarded today. But the
lesson is still there. The modern world prepares for the
coming of Christ, if it prepares at all, in a way very different
from the rigour of John. It is a noisy, busy world in which we
live, centred on material gifts and material pleasure. In fact
it is a world which loves itself so well it has no time to love
God. Into this atmosphere must flow John's spirit of silence
and penance and humility. Once it has flowed to us, it can
only flow on by our example.

Therefore, the Church brings us back each year to the
same considerations, as old and as new as love itself. But,
since each year in the Old Testament came nearer to the
fullness of time, we too each year come nearer to the fullness
of God's time, when he will call us once and for all to judgement.

Here and now is the moment for us to prepare. Now, not
tomorrow. It takes courage to learn John's lesson, with
humility to face our failings; hence the demand for our decrease that we may better accept the outpouring of God's
merciful love—

> *Of all man's clotted clay the dingiest clot?*
> *Alack, thou knowest not,*
> *How little worthy of any love thou art!*
> *Whom wilt thou find to love ignoble thee*
> *Save me, save only Me?*[1]

[1] Francis Thompson, *The Hound of Heaven.*

XI

PREPARATION—THE WOMAN

IT is difficult to know quite how much of a muddle man's mind is in about his preparation for "inheriting the kingdom". Perhaps there is just that feeling of darkness and obscurity which so often surrounds us in this world, when we cannot see which way to go . . . or why.

That is the muddle of God's plan for the world. Not that God is muddled, but he chooses to work out our salvation on such a scale that we cannot stand sufficiently far back to get an idea of the whole. Corners of pictures, without relation to the whole, can look unbalanced, unsymmetrical, hideous. This needs great stress in these days of Mathematics for the Million, ready-made scientific answers for all problems.

There is no answer to individual problems in individual lives, except in relation to the Providence of God, who wills all things sweetly. God's providence means God's economy, and God does not waste. We must cling to this truth with increasing tenacity, because here at least it is stranger than fiction. I mean this. God's providence appears madness to men. And our individual parts in the redemption are equally mad, very often. For instance, here and now your husband has run away with someone else; it is not right, but God is not wasting it; if you sit and say, if he had not gone all would have been lovely, well so it might; but you are expected here and now to get up and go on living, because that is the will of God. You who always wanted to go into a convent or monastery! You must go on in the rush of life, and if God wants you inside four walls, he will make sure everything works out to get you there. You are convinced you are called to write, to act, to teach—you may find these are the only things you are never allowed to do. You cannot get close to God because there is so much else going on and no time to pray, you must learn that the acceptance of the ceaseless rush is your *Fiat*.

There is a depth of understanding of our insufficiency, a wealth of faith and humility to be drawn from the virgin's well at Nazareth. We spoke before of time and timelessness. But though it is easy to speak, it is more difficult to apply the principles to our lives. God does not worry about days, weeks or years. To him a day is as a thousand years and a thousand years as a day.

Perhaps the best way of impressing this upon ourselves is to study God's choice of Mary. He waited all those thousands of years after Adam to find a soul who was fitted bodily and spiritually to offer him a home. After all these ages, he created one soul and preserved it immaculate, thus using his eternity to full advantage; for he made her immaculate by anticipating the redemption in time, taking her, as it were, into his eternity, redeeming her, and placing her, as one born out of due time, in the world of sin, sinless. Only by the merits of the son she was to bear was she born immaculate. And it was not apparent to the world. She was not hailed as a freak. No one knew of Mary as worthy of record in history. Her parents dedicated her to the service of the temple, according to tradition . . . but that was all, and not uncommon. The mark of God did not shine on her forehead as a brand. And she herself knew nothing of her destiny.

How interesting this is to us. God does not in normal circumstances tell us what he has planned for us. We are left to find out. We live according to his rule, and it manifests itself or remains hidden in varying ways. We may expect, but we do not get, a revelation about whom we are to marry, what order we are to join. We work out our salvation, just as Mary did. Her choice like that of so many was direct service in the temple, as the fullest way she could give herself to him, consecrating her most cherished possession to him . . . her virginity. All down the ages, theological opinion has endorsed the idea that, objectively speaking, virginity is a higher state than marriage but the will of God for each individual varies, so that subjectively marriage may well be the higher state for a given person. Mary saw clearly that for her from both viewpoints virginity was the more excellent way.

The great thing we must see here is that when God began to reveal what he wanted to do to her, Mary was perplexed at the suggestion. Most women of Israel considered it a stigma to be without child . . . look only at the example of Elizabeth. It was a humiliation to be barren. Not only was marriage robbed of its fruit, but God's displeasure seemed to hover over the barren woman, for in each heart deep down was the hope of bearing the redeemer. How very different was Mary's outlook. When Gabriel says, "Thou shalt conceive in thy womb and bring forth a son," she replies, "How can this be done? I know not man."

What an amazing statement this is. The daughter of the house of David is offered the Motherhood of God, and she holds it at arm's length, seeming to prefer her virginity, the way she had always seen as her approach to God. There is no refusal to obey, for the angel essentially made a proposal, it being part of the plan of God for the free soul to accept freely . . . the whole of God's plan depending again upon the choice of a creature. Yet at the same time she stresses that she has seen the immense value of her virginity, and even the priceless lure of the Motherhood of God is not sufficient to change her course. To us poor creatures who would have been overwhelmed by the apparition alone, this seeming preference is astonishing.

It did not, however, astonish God. Rather it was the final factor sealing Mary in her part, marking her off as purest of creatures. She who was unwilling to risk her virginity even for this highest honour was outstandingly the soul to accept most worthily the task of bearing God's son.

In our startlingly immoral world today, when virginity is lost by many while still so young, when the streets of London are thronged by ten thousand prostitutes, seeking an all too numerous and willing clientele, when purity is despised and immorality crowned festive king—this is just the time to see what virginity meant to Mary. Her strength of faith which had led her through life said she must not yield her virginity, for any purpose. Humble and insufficient of herself, her faith made her so strong she could go to any lengths, realizing that God's Providence was going on before her.

And therefore, as much as anything else, her question was simply a test of Gabriel's origin. As she was seeking God's will, any messenger giving it to her would be well received. Whatever God said must be accepted, once proved to come from God, for she was to be the mother of the son of whom it was written that he was "obedient unto death, even the death of the Cross". We can see this penetrating question testing the archangel, because her schooling had been in the Scriptures and she knew as well or better than the other women of her race that Isaias said, "A virgin shall conceive and bear a son." Therefore as soon as Gabriel is tested and found true, her acceptance is immediate and complete and for that reason full of humility and joy.

One great lesson comes to us at once. She did not run round telling people. She was given the sign of Elizabeth, and so went to see her, to see the fulfilment of God's will and to help her in any way possible. It is now not for her to worry about details of how it shall all come into being. God has said it, our duty is to go on with our present-moment occupation, leaving to God his own fulfilment. The world would have done nothing without a proof. Mary did nothing exceptional, because there was nothing exceptional to be done. She lived normally. She gives us a signal example of her absolute confidence in God's Providence; we are God's children too, and God does not abandon children . . . no . . . not even when they abandon him. His hands, however, are tied by his children, so that he cannot keep his promises unless they follow his will, for his will is our sanctification. Deliberately choosing to flout his will is automatically to choose perdition.

The main difficulty which prevents us from grasping our dependence upon God's Providence and our happiness in doing God's will in this . . . our failure to take God at his word, our failure to realize there is no limit to the amount we can do, supported by him. Advent presses the point upon us, if we have eyes to see and ears to hear. From reading the Gospels we know a little of the madness of John the Baptist, crying against the world to save the world. We know too the other end of the tale, the utter improvidence of God's birth as man, leading to the penury of burial in someone else's grave.

But now we want to study the trial of Mary's faith, the poverty of spirit which produced the *Magnificat*. The whole story is a contradiction, or rather a paradox. And it is necessary for us to see it in relation to our own position.

The spiritual life is never one where we reach such a state that we are free from trial and hardship. We live by faith, children of God, insufficient of ourselves, leaning on him. If ever anyone came to a close union of spirit with God in this world it was Mary. Already she had been told by the angel that she was "full of grace", she has accepted the position of Mother of God, she has been obedient in all things. Surely she deserves a reward from God of peace and plenty, but instead of this we find that he has placed her in an impossible position. He has given her a child, when she is unmarried. All Nazareth knows she is a virgin, though espoused to Joseph. Indeed part of Joseph's deep love for Mary must rest upon her purity of soul and body. Imagine the feelings of doubt, of dismay, when there appear in the figure of his young spouse the unmistakable signs of pregnancy. How he must have tried to put off the idea, until there could no longer be room for doubt. He knew nothing of the angel's visit or of God's command that she shall bear a child.

And Mary did not tell him; God had announced it to her; had he wanted Joseph to know, he would have told him. Until he did, she was content to await his will, knowing he would not let her down. She, Mary, had no message to give. Nothing, humanly, seems worse than this situation. For Mary, it was sad to see the perplexity of Joseph; she knew the law of stoning which became her due if she was discovered bearing child. And Joseph was caught on both sides. The law demanded that he denounce Mary as a sinner, but his heart and his knowledge of her denied the possibility which his eyes proclaimed. In all this, both show the calm tranquillity which we would so soon have lacked. They go on with their daily lives, and when there is a fear that the villagers will suspect Mary, Joseph wishes to take a middle course by hiding her away. The trial perhaps was greater for Joseph, but then he had to be such a selfless solid rock that every test must be made of his faith before the child came.

Humanly, we cannot understand the folly of God's plan, his seeming improvidence in leaving this awful secret separating Joseph and Mary. Apply it quickly to our own life. How many times do we see things happening which appear impossibly out of line with our own idea of the way things should work out. As soon as darkness falls, as soon as we are left alone, desolate, we begin to wilt. Despairing of God's power to help us, we begin to make friends of mammon, excusing ourselves to the public, explaining away a hard doctrine or a fault into which we have fallen, a difficult position to which we must cling, a rocky dogma, which is decried as intolerant.

And so throughout Advent there are continual examples in the liturgy of the uttermost bounds of confidence to which, and beyond which, God expects us to go. Humanly it is much too far. In theory we then bring God in to help us carry on. In theory. But God is not a theory, God is being, and being is very practical. We can live beautifully confident until the test hits us. But what then? Take the example of a family with several children, not a large income and the possibility of another child. The world says that is madness and must be stopped. Or take any other example of difficulty at work, in the office or factory, trouble in the home, tension. Often we feel it is madness to carry on.

The answer God points out through Mary, in the words of Christ, "My meat is to do the will of him who sent me." It could not be clearer. His will is the only thing which matters, to me, the doing of his will is the only thing that matters in my life; but it is his will, and so it must be his life, not my will and my life. Harping back to John the Baptist it is: "He must increase but I must decrease." This means complete obedience and humble acceptance even of human impossibility.

Mary was completely humble and completely obedient. She knew she was dealing with God. What is more to the point she behaved accordingly. Once the will of God was established, there was nothing to fear. Until it had been established, she lived ordinarily according to what she knew of his will, through the Scriptures, and prayer. Her *Magnificat* is the forerunner of St Paul's, "I can do all things in him who strengtheneth me." Of herself, all that was required was the continuation of life as it had been lived until that time. God had spoken; therefore God would see to it that the stage was set for the accomplishment of his word. She did not sit idle, with hands folded, waiting. But she waited with hands busy, working and praying. This was a full-time occupation, having Elizabeth in her confinement, and the household duties at Nazareth, no more glamorous than any household chores, but none the less necessary for the salvation of the world.

All of which teaches us this. Here and now, for some reason best known to himself, God is allowing you to sit reading. Moreover he has allowed the whole world to be as it is. That does not mean that we continue to sit for the rest of time. We can see, for instance, even from our small knowledge, that some of the world is not doing God's will, and so we have no excuse for idleness, for letting that state of affairs go on. But in any case, whether we are rich or poor, married or single, professional or amateur, beginning or ending our life, if we are trying to live in accordance with God's will, we are aiming at perfection, we are following Mary as she follows Christ. And therefore, instead of having jagged ends spoiling the pattern of our days, everything fits into place, for everything, from the early ringing of the alarm to the last weary step into bed at night is an expression of God's providence over us, loving us, and should be in return an expression of our trust in that providence, loving him.

It does not really matter how silly the things seem to be which God demands. If he were to put you in the position of Prime Minister tomorrow, you could do it, with him behind you. If he gives you another child when you cannot provide for the ones you have, go on with your life, obeying his commandments, not worrying. "All will be well, and all will be well and all manner of thing will be well," as Juliana of Norwich puts it. You will never get a greater trial of faith than Mary and Joseph had—never. And if you did, God would not let you down. It is simple to make and accept that statement when there is no immediate crisis. It remains all right if it is forgotten five minutes later. But all the same, it is much more real and immediate than we like to think. For you will be asked absurdities as Mary was. Have a child and remain a virgin? . . . what nonsense! . . . but *Fiat mihi secundum verbum tuum* is the answer. The world scoffs. It will scoff at you. And therefore please be determined about three things in life:

You are going to follow John the Baptist to the madness of the desert.

You are going to follow Mary to the improvidence of the *Magnificat*.

You are going to follow Christ to the folly of the Cross.

But you will do this only in so far as you are fully conscious of the fact that nothing is impossible to God, in proportion as you are not only conscious of this, but living that consciousness in your life. You cannot accept this as a theory. It is not a theory, any more than prayer is a theory. It is of all practices practical. Until you *know* this from experience, you will convince no one. Until you *know* God will not let you down—which each man does know though he will not admit it in practice—until you *know* it, you cannot stop grasping wildly at material straws. You need aids in life? Of course. That is why God gives them. But he gives what you need, not necessarily what you want. He has anticipated every need. It is guaranteed that if you do your small share, he does his big one, eternally, because he loves you with an everlasting love.

The *fiat* has to be made with Mary, understanding the depth of poverty from which man cries. Then it can be more truly realized that Christ has already heard the spoken or unspoken prayer when he said, "Come to me, all ye who labour and are heavy burdened, and I will refresh you."

To accept this is to live by faith, wrought with love. It is a case of giving by accepting what is taken away, accepting what has never been given, accepting the love of God:

All which I took from thee I did but take
 not for thy harms
But just that thou might'st seek it in my arms.
All which thy child's mistake
Fancies as lost, I have stored for thee at home:
Rise, clasp my hand, and come.[1]

[1] Francis Thompson, *The Hound of Heaven.*

XII

MOTHER OF THE YEAR

POPE PIUS XII, from his accession to the See of Peter, has continually turned the eyes of the faithful to the unique place of the Mother of God in Christianity. He calls on his children to increase their devotion to our Lady, stressing the message which has been given at each recent apparition of the Blessed Virgin—prayer and penance. Everyone will surely admit that if the sanctity of each individual member of Christ's Church were developed and intensified, the effect upon the world would be immeasurable.

Here it is therefore necessary to be sure of our distinction between theology and devotion. The former has God and his revelation, the deposit of faith, for its subject matter. It is a solid, unchanging treasure, which may be understood more fully as time goes on, but has the constancy of Christ; it is the precious stone whose beauty is penetrated more and more deeply by the bright light of faith.

Devotion is more subjective. It is based upon the great articles of faith, but because it is the expression of ordinary people's love for the beliefs and persons they hold dear, it may assume different forms at different times. Thus we all believe in the Immaculate Conception, upon which new lustre has shone during the past century. But not all of us are bound to say or even to like the Rosary, though many millions do; for this is a devotion and its popularity may ebb or flow, be localized or fill the world with Hail Marys; at the present time, not least because of the emphasis used by our Lady at Lourdes and Fatima, the Rosary is a daily devotion among Catholics. Its efficacy as a form of prayer we have already considered in an earlier chapter. Perhaps here we should do well to understand how closely it can be linked to the story of our Lord's life as we meditate upon the great truths of the Incarnation.

The Church has a very beautiful liturgical cycle, which carries us through the story of the world's redemption from Advent to Easter, from Pentecost back to Advent again. It is precisely because the whole year concentrates upon our redemption that we find so many feasts of our Lady up and down the calendar. God chose to redeem us by sending his Son to become man through the motherhood of Mary. We are not theorizing on what course God might have taken, but we are regarding the fact of the Incarnation. The whole basis for the doctrine of the Immaculate Conception rests on this great condescension of God that he "did not disdain the Virgin's womb". Mary was a human creature descended from Adam, and so liable on conception to inherit Adam's sin. God's favour was to preserve her from it by a redemptive act that anticipated the work of her divine Son. Truly human and truly redeemed, the Fathers loved to name her as the second Eve, while the Church rejoices to echo the angelic salutation, "Hail, full of grace." It is no wonder, then, that the feast of "our tainted nature's solitary boast" is kept at the opening of the liturgical year.

We pass on to the fulfilment of Isaias' prophecy by celebrating the birth of Christ at Christmas. Too often, nowadays, the child forgets his mother when his own birthday comes round. But can a Christian celebrate Christmas with any understanding, with any appreciation of the tremendous truth that lies behind this feast, if in worshipping God-made-man he neglects the Mother who conceived him in human flesh and gave him birth? In fact, we mark the occasion by a Mass at Midnight, in which the priest says: "Keeping that

most holy night in which the spotless virginity of the Blessed
Mary brought forth a Saviour to this world;" and then pro-
ceeds to make Christ truly present upon the altar. Our Lady,
who of all human beings alone lived through the entire
earthly life of Christ in complete union with him, justly
increases our love for him as we see her there, Mother most
pure. Indeed what an indictment she is of the modern world.
Pure in the midst of impurity, she shows at once the fruitful-
ness of virginity and the chastity of married life. At Christmas
may men grasp the idea:

> *That Christ from this creative purity*
> *Came forth your sterile appetites to scorn.*[1]

She stands as a contradiction to those who claim the impossibility of self-discipline. In an age which has seen the great
advance of women, she marks heights to which no woman
has ever risen. She is a challenge to her sex to uphold the
nobility of woman in an ignoble world.

The world's new year begins as the Church is quietly pointing out the task of the Mother. She not only begets her Child;
she also brings him to maturity. Bethlehem, Egypt, Nazareth,
these only make the busy clamour of the modern world a
greater contrast by their silence. Yet here, within the family,
Christ grew. We should not forget Mary as a human mother.
If we picture her always as "a queen most womanly", we
must see her too with her back aching, her eyes tired, her
fingers cracked with washing. We must see her in anxiety, in
poverty, in aridity. She shares everything a human mother
undergoes, except that she, like her Son, does not sin. A
family must have a mother. It does not need modern psychology to tell us that. In turning to Mary, we only do what
Christ did, with the instinct of a child. To banish her, to be
self-conscious about her, to say she is a barrier to the Son,

[1] G. K. Chesterton.

this is all unnatural. Here the East speaks as plainly as the West:

> To whatever religion he may belong, an Oriental will hardly feel at home while there is no mother. That is one reason why, although I was a Methodist for nineteen years, I somehow missed the Mother. Was not God enough? Of course He is; nay, more than enough. But it is precisely His will that we should adopt the Mother of Christ to be our Mother. So long as this will of His is not complied with, our filial piety toward Him is not complete.[1]

To think of Jesus, then, is to accept the presence of Mary. With this in mind, the Church takes us through Lent to the great redemptive act itself. "There stood by the Cross. . . ." In a sense this is a summary of the part of woman. Mother still, Mary is now Mother of Sorrows. She like all women has been born to suffer with a greater capacity than man; she is of her nature more contemplative, more able to wait patiently on God, more ready to say "Be it done unto me according to thy word". Christ was the man of sorrows; in these Mary shared as only she could share, the sinless Mother:

> *You saw her everywhere.*
> *With the people and a little apart from the people.*
> *Under the porticoes, under the arcades, in drafty places. . . .*
> *And she had also gone up to Calvary.*[2]

The lesson for all mankind is the lesson of the Cross. Mary learned it fully. When we stand in Passiontide once more at the foot of the Cross and examine the world wounds which we bear, rather than getting depressed, we can think that at this very moment of deep suffering, Mary was given her cross and her crown—the Motherhood of men. Looking at Golgotha

[1] Dr. John Wu, *Beyond East and West* (Sheed and Ward)
[2] Charles Péguy, *The Passion of Our Lady*, tr. by Julian Green (Pantheon Books Inc.).

with its three crosses, gaunt against the sky like some horrid sin caricaturing nature, we cannot neglect the figure of the woman, the mother, waiting there, any more than we can ignore her at the crib. The whole world turns between these two poles of Bethlehem and Jerusalem. How very right and beautiful it is that God, ennobling man's nature by becoming man, should at the same time ennoble woman by making her a fit person to build up his human body from her own.

If Mary shared in Calvary, she was surely not neglected at the Resurrection. There are so many things we might like to know, which the Evangelists did not think it necessary to relate. To kneel early one Easter Sunday morning by the Holy Sepulchre was for me an invitation to be distracted into wondering about the first sight of her Son that Mary had after that dreadful Friday afternoon. When, where and how? It might be nice to know, but one is always reminded of Christ's attitude that human joys and sorrows, human values as a whole are put in perspective by the basic necessity, "Blessed are they that hear the word of God and keep it."

Still now, after the Resurrection, Mary continues to keep God's word. Any human plan we might conceive would make provision for our Lady, her task well done, to live in peace or to go immediately to heaven. Yet Christ leaves her on earth for the birth of the Church, and to assist by her prayers its first movements of life. Is it not the tradition that her powerful prayers were a great source of grace in those times? At this season of the year, after Whitsuntide, we trail off into pilgrimages to Lourdes, political crises, summer holidays, a succession of Sundays after Pentecost, droughts, bank holiday disasters, liberally interspersed with crime, violence and murder. This is the time to remember that Mary was left as Mother of Men. Her mission continues. Not only is devotion to her great in Christ's Church, but she herself encourages it by appearing at Lourdes and Fatima. She urges us to greater efforts in prayer; she tells selfish man to be mortified. These things remind us that, whether we like it or not, Mary is playing a part in God's plan.

There is nothing new in what she says. Again and again it is the message of her divine Son: pray, do penance! When so much emphasis is being put upon standards of living and the alleviation of bodily pain, our Lady gives us her crucified Son. There is no easy way. An endless round of compromise leads nowhere; peace conferences come and go; social legislation gets to the stage of nightmare. Without God the world turns values topsy-turvy.

Into the middle of August, then, there bursts, not a declaration of war, but a shout of the Church triumphant— *Assumpta est Maria in Coelum!* It echoes through the casinos, along the beaches; it drowns the blare of music at the holiday camp; it causes the harvester to pause at his stooking, the worker at his lathe in the factory; it throws a new light of hope into the concentration camp, and causes the proud materialist a misgiving shown in anger. It is the cry of this century, because this century no longer respects the soul or the body, no longer owns God. It sets up for us as Catholics the goal of our "vale of tears", and it makes startlingly clear to those outside the Church that Catholic belief is as strong and sure and full of love as when Christ preached in Palestine and Mary stood by the Cross. It sweeps us on to Autumn, almost to the entry of another liturgical year, where we meet once more the fundamental truth round which all revolves: God became man, and Mary was his Mother.

There is a lovely passage in Cardinal Newman with which we can aptly summarize the position of our Lady in God's plan. Perhaps if we could only be a little more human in our approach to God, we might realize better His infinite consideration for our own weak human nature:

I recollect the strange emotion which took by surprise men and women, young and old, when, at the time of the Coronation of our present Queen, they gazed on the figure· of one so like a child, so small, so tender, so shrinking, who had been exalted to so great an inheritance and so vast a rule, who was in such contrast in her own person to the solemn pageant which centred in her. Could it be otherwise with the spectators, if they had human affection? And did not the All-wise know the human heart when He took to Himself a Mother? Did He not anticipate our emotion at the sight of such an exaltation in one so simple and so lowly? . . . If she is not to attract our homage, why did He make her solitary in her greatness amid His vast creation? If it be idolatry in us to let our affections respond to our faith, He would not have made her what she is . . . but He sent His Prophet to announce to us "A Virgin shall conceive and bear a Son, and they shall call his name Emmanuel", and we have the same warrant for hailing her as God's Mother, as we have for adoring Him as God.[1]

[1] Cardinal Newman, *The New Eve.*

XIII

APPROACHING THE PASSION

WHEN dealing with the subject of meditation in an earlier chapter, mention was made of the pictures which could be formed in the mind from scenes in the life of our Lord, and so on. St Ignatius called this part of the meditation the composition of place.

It was not until I came to spend a year in Palestine that I began to appreciate how such a background could help. I began to try to visit the various places as the appropriate Gospel or feast day arrived in the Church's calendar. It became not only a fascinating attempt at reconstruction, but also a most useful source of meditation. Admittedly this has been scorned by some to whom I have suggested it, but I continue to urge people to gain a more living reality on visiting any place which has been made holy by its past associations. Whether it is Naim or Damascus, Assisi or Alverna, Lourdes, Fatima or Walsingham, all these have lived, as it were, a holy life in the past.

Now, necessarily, the ideas in the next few pages are only my ideas. They were picked up when I was not gathering material for a book, but serving as one of the "rude and scoffing soldiery". Yet they still manage to bring alive again the various scenes as they crop up each year. Surely, one object of the liturgical cycle is to encourage us to use our minds in this way, and meditation, particularly upon the Passion, has always been a basic ingredient of the life of the saints. It should, then, be possible for us to take advantage also.

To show you what I mean, I am going to say something about Passiontide in Palestine. It is, however, necessary to set the scene by beginning a little before the entry into Jerusalem to get an idea of what might be called the psychology of the country which built up into the last few days and prepared the way for the final act in man's redemption.

We must look a minute at Galilee, for instance, before we "go up to Jerusalem". Perhaps our English climate gives us the wrong impression from the beginning. The Palestine climate is well in advance of ours. Thus you can come from the coast by Mount Carmel into the plain of Jezrael or Esdraelon, and at once you are struck by the aptness of one of Chesterton's queries, "Have you ever known what it is like to walk along a road in such a frame of mind that you thought you might meet God at any turn of the path?" As you pass Little Hermon, where nestles Naim, and on whose side is Endor, where the witch came from, you can say "Jesus Christ stood hereabouts"; as you cross over towards the mountainous molehill of Tabor, you can say, "Our Lord was transfigured here" . . . this is not the passing thunder of a prophet, this is not the mere relic of a saint, no vision of transient mortal glory, but the presence of God made man.

In the rare morning light in Galilee you can see the Gospel live; afar off, Tabor rises like a carbuncle on a man's face. But it is not this which takes your breath away. Rather it is the brilliant cloud, its edges tinged with gold, which drapes the summit, so that unconsciously you find yourself quoting: "And as he was yet speaking, behold a bright cloud over-shadowed them, and lo! a voice out of the cloud saying: This is my beloved Son in whom I am well pleased. Hear ye him." And then if you climb the precipitous winding path to the top, the Franciscans will give you a glass of cool red wine, and allow you to walk under the growing heat of the sun, in the rosemary scented garden, in and out among the shady olive trees, hearing the drone of many bees, feeling yourself half a mile in the sky.

But you cannot linger, for not far away, little Nazareth calls you. Surely it is the most captivating of towns, set in the hills, high above the plain; I felt certain each time I went up to Nazareth that, despite the rejection, our Lord and our Lady loved it still, to the end, partly because of the memory of St Joseph, partly in the way in which we love the place in which we spend our early years; no matter how it treats us afterwards, that love stays on. Thus, unlike Capharnaum or Corozain, Nazareth was not destroyed; Nazareth did not understand, just because it was the Prophet's own city; for this very reason it was excused, a wonderful lesson to us of the way in which God forgives those he loves; and so he spared it the toils that Jerusalem suffered, or even the tragic epics of the Crusaders at Bethlehem. The peace lives on, or did a few years ago, the peace of the family; carpenters still ply their trade by the wayside, their shops open to the street; here humble folk stand to gossip, while grubby infants sprawl upon the ground's carpet of shavings and sawdust.

But what is all this about, you will say? What have I come to see? And with a shout of joy I can say, "Nothing more, just this. . . ." That is the supreme delight, that is where you learn to understand the Gospel, not in this particular building, not in this relic of our Lady's veil. Here on the hilltop, so often spoken of by our Lord, you feel the good tidings of the Gospel, just as later in Jerusalem or by the Dead Sea, you can breathe the evil blowing in your nostrils. Here the colossal fact is that the memory leaps at sudden glimpses; a maid carrying water in a pot on her head, a sparrow twittering in the cyprus, children sitting in the market-place, who crying to their companions say, "We have piped to you and you have not danced." Here you get all this, because Jesus loved the small things of the world, which are really the big things, if we can only see it that way . . .

> *Good news, but if you ask me what it is, I know not;*
> *It is a track of feet in the snow,*
> *It is a lantern showing a path,*
> *It is a door set open.*

So, through the hills of Galilee, you feel like singing all the way, especially at this time of year, with the crimson purple of anemones, the pale sweetness of narcissi, the blood red splendour of poppies sweeping along from spur to spur, to fall away quite suddenly till you see there below in blue serenity the palm clustered shore of Lake Genasereth, the Sea of Galilee. This was the way our Lord came; this was the way the Ruler from Capharnaum took as he went home rejoicing that his son lived. It is an incredibly lovely sight, cut out of the earth below the level of the sea, while beyond the gaunt cliffs of Gadera, down which the swine once rushed to drown, stand now a sharp ridge, softening into the shimmering desert, that vast Syrian plateau leading to fabulous Bagdad. This, all this, was what Christ left when he went up to Jerusalem.

We do not have to minimize the humanity of Christ. Many would overemphasize it; but let us do justice to God made man. He had the heart of a man, which felt and loved as a man. You have only to read the parables to see the love for the flowers of the field, for the harvest, for the people round about him. Apart from any dread of the Passion, he had to feel this parting from the Galilee he loved so well.

As we follow our Lord to Jerusalem, we choose to go by the road that leads through Samaria, and it gives us an opportunity for seeing the way that even the Old Testament continues to live today, and so I make no excuse for including here an impression of the Samaritan Passover, kept each year on the Holy Mount Gerizim, towering as it does above the well where Jesus asked water from the Samaritan woman. As you know, the first Passover was kept at God's order when the Jews were to flee from Egypt; and to cause consternation, the Angel of God was sent to kill the first-born of all the Egyptian families, while the followers of Moses were spared, by the sign of a bloody cross put upon the lintels of their tents. Even today, this foreshadowing of the Passion is re-enacted to the minutest detail, though the Samaritans fail to see the fulfilment in the death of Christ upon the Cross. This then is how it seems to happen.

The tumbling roofs and jagged walls of Samaria were kissed by the golden red of the evening sun; from the minaret, the muezzin called to prayer the few faithful Moslems lingering in the empty streets, a call which re-echoed across the narrow pass, struck the mountain barrier to the north, and wreathed fantastic sounds among the clinging olive groves and vineyards on the slopes.

They say that one of the angels, who was charged by God with the building of the world, was passing over towards Africa, bearing a load of rocks, all done up in his own heavenly blanket, and intended to be scattered through the length and breadth of that great continent; alas, one corner of the blanket slipped from his grasp, and the whole descended in glittering, thudding, bounding cascades on Palestine. Certainly, Joseph Ben Ackman, the Samaritan, thought the angel might have been more careful. It had been a long trying day; he had been up early for his journey to the holy mountain, and his brother's ass had been particularly obstinate, until he had finally decided to leave it tethered at the bottom, near the town, while he climbed on up and up. As he climbed, he was forever stubbing his toes against the boulders, and each time his mind and words were out of keeping with his holy pilgrimage. But now, ahead, he could see the white tents of his brethren, scattered near the sacred spot.

He must hurry, for at any moment the watchman on the peak would catch the first yellow fullness of the moon, as she sailed up across the Transjordan hills, and by that time, he must be there.

A few minutes more and he was among them. How few they were; why since last year they had dwindled; but this was no time for self-pity. Even as he drew his breath in panting gasps, the pale figure of the High Priest stepped forward, accompanied by his minions. Each was clad traditionally in the flowing white, each grasped a tall staff in his left hand, while in the right gleamed a beautiful curve of sharpened steel. Slowly they approached the woolly wide-eyed animals . . . slowly, for they waited till the watchman should cry the moon. Listen to the Book of Exodus . . .

On the tenth day of this month, let every man take a lamb by their families and houses. . . .

And it shall be a lamb without blemish, a male of one year. . . .

And you shall keep it until the fourteenth day of this month; and the whole multitude of the children of Israel shall sacrifice it in the evening. . . .

At last the shrill wailing cry from the peak, a hundred heads, a hundred pairs of eyes sought the queen of the night as she rode her chariot into the sky; then a dozen priestly arms raised high, fell plunging into the yielding necks, the life-blood spattered the goblets held ready, spattered the virgin albs, and the quivering victims died.

The solemn hush ended, and Ben Ackman with the rest broke into the wild rhythmic chant. The High Priest, taking the goblet in his hands and followed by the crowd, moved away from the dead carcasses of the lambs, towards his people's tents . . .

And they shall take the blood thereof, and put it on both the side posts, and on the upper doorposts of the houses. . . .

Thus they did, obeying the letter of the law, and then hurried back; some of them skinned the lambs, others built fires, yet others collected the bitter herbs required. All the while, a high discordant wail continued, as by the light of their torches and the moon, staves grasped in their hands, a few of the priests stood nearby, chanting their ancient prayers. Ben Ackman found himself feverishly collecting all burnable furse and scrub from round about; and then with others he lit the fires at the bottom of the round, ten foot deep ovens, cut, well-like, into the ground. The flames from the brushwood leapt into the night, catching the glint of knives, as they gutted the bodies; jumping fantastic figures on the hillside, shadows of lambs hanging transfixed upon rude wooden crosses, of gory hands depositing the entrails on another fire, flickering from bush to rock, until the stench of burning offal mingled in the air with the rise and fall of the litany. To Joseph, all seemed ready for the next part of the ceremony, and indeed he could soon see the carcasses, whole from head to legs, not a bone broken, placed upon the trestles, could see many sinewy arms seize lumps of crude salt, could see them rub and pummel the still-warm flesh, great beads of perspiration standing from their foreheads, as the torches danced in the moonlight. . . .

And this day shall be a great feast for a memorial to you; and you shall keep it, a feast of the Lord, in your generations, with an everlasting observance. . . .

The oven fire, by this time, had died to a mass of glowing embers, though the heat was still intense. Joseph Ben Ackman, his task accomplished, drew back from the edge of the oven, for the eager crowd was straining to the very brink. And now, at a sign from the High Priest, the lambs without blemish were borne through the air, until those who carried them rested the bases of the spits round the oven, in a circle on the ground. Immediately, they broke the silence again, and the answer was flung back by the people. Joseph felt a sudden swirl of energy and feeling rise within him, as the whole body of faithful swayed to the rhythm, and then at once, with a wild gesture, the bearers raised their burdens and thrust them down into the glowing hole in the ground. This done, many willing hands threw in the bitter herbs on top, and sealed the oven with undergrowth and mud.

The chant fell to a croon, which the women took up from their tents. And so they waited, Joseph Ben Ackman and his Samaritan brethren, last of a dying, despised race, who still bore witness to the Redeemer, whose coming they had not eyes to see—for did not the book tell them to await the cooking of the lambs. . . .

> And thus shall you eat; you shall gird your reins, and you shall have shoes on your feet, holding staves in your hands, and you shall eat in haste; for it is the Phase (that is the Passage) of the Lord.

This, I hope, will give you some idea of two things. Firstly, there is a very ancient form of worship which still exists among the Samaritans, dating back in its main form to the Exodus, yet it is not the correct form, now. The Samaritan, even in the days of our Lord, was a despised person, an outcast from the Jewish religion. There were errors and heresies in Judaism as there are today in Christianity. Yet God allowed the cockle to grow on with the true crop until the harvest. And secondly, in the very heresy can be seen the deadening effect, the branch cut away from the vine, not unlike the situation in the Orthodox Churches today . . . the lack of vitality refuses all development and leads to eventual decay.

Against this, look at the living faith and liturgy of the Church. And do not be content simply to look. Get down to it, get on with it, and so absorb its vital spirit.

XIV

THE WAY OF THE CROSS

IT was the Jewish form of this Pasch that our Lord went up to
Jerusalem to celebrate with his disciples. And so, as all places
have their seasons, we must go to Jerusalem at Passiontide,
for there alone can we get the local colour of the Passion. I
often felt unhappy at entering Jerusalem. I do not think it
was only the fact that I went without a military leave or duty
pass. I think it must have had the same sort of atmosphere at
the preaching of the Gospel, but then atmospheres are very
subjective, so I may have imagined the whole thing. At any
rate, I found Galilee simple, open, full of the beauty of
nature; so too, indeed, are the surroundings of Jerusalem;
but the city itself is close, jealous, shut up in its own thoughts
and schemes . . . it has the bitter hypocritical taint of the
Pharisee and Sadducee.

Yet it is that very atmosphere which helps to picture the
Passion. If you ever go to Jerusalem, try to go in Holy Week;
the experience must live with you as long as you breathe. I do
not pretend that it looks today as it did in the days of Christ,
for we all know that much of the old city is buried twenty feet
below the present level, in order to fulfil the prophecy that
not a stone should be left upon a stone. Indeed, the whole has
changed again since I was there, in renewed warfare; but a
few years ago, once you had left the glaring white square
buildings, so unimaginative, that boast the New Jerusalem,
once you are within the walls, you are borne back into the
days of Geoffrey de Bouillon and Richard Coeur de Lion.
There are many disappointments, as well as pleasures; for

instance, the Church of the Holy Sepulchre, built by the Crusaders, looks today like the beginning of a Bailey Bridge, profuse in steel girders as though someone had put them up and forgotten to take them away. So the most hallowed spot in Christendom stands, or rather totters, in dereliction.

What is there then to draw the mind and heart to Jerusalem? It is just that possibility for the ordinary person of making the Gospel live. Until we are capable of the higher unions of prayer, we need some of St Ignatius' composition of place; we like images to some extent, and to some extent they are good. I cannot attempt to do what some writers have taken books to do, and failed. I want only to say that the whole of the liturgy is made, not to be a dead thing, cut off from the people, unintelligible. It is meant to live, to sweep up the laity as well as the clergy in its beauty and mystery and magnificence. That is why the Holy Father has allowed the reintroduction of the night ceremonies for Holy Saturday. That is why, in Jerusalem, you have such a wonderful chance to take your place beside Christ in his Passion during Holy Week. For the basis of Catholicism is to live in Christ, while Christ lives in you; it is more than that, it is to spread that life of Christ to those round about you, but that, too, you can only do, when you are filled with Christ yourself. See then how the Passion lives again in Jerusalem.

The beginning of the Passion is triumph, the way that Judas thought it should be worked, the way so obviously wrong to the Son of God, the way we have to learn all our lives to avoid, that is the way of praise and power and earthly success. Each Palm Sunday, then, the people gather on the brow of the hill called Olivet, and carrying palms and olives, great branches of them, they wind their route down into the valley, past the spot where Jesus wept over Jerusalem. There it lies in all its magnificence, the noble buildings of the temple dominating the foreground. Then on down the slippery stony path, until they reach the brook Kedron, running down among the tombs of the Prophets, down the Vale of Josaphat, where the Last Judgement is awaited by the forerunners of Christ. Then they climb again, waving their greenery, shouting in triumph, singing Hosannas, as they enter the gates of the city. The sun beats down, the olive trees shimmer silvery in the hot breeze, the people rejoice that Jerusalem has recognized its King.

But there was still that day or two to pass before Christ was to die, and during those days, he taught in the temple, and walked each evening back over Olivet to Bethany, to the house of Simon, to Martha and Mary. Here on his way, he saw and cursed the fig tree, so that it withered away, and so today you can imagine the feeling of Christ as you climb the rough paths under the hot spring sun; and you can see how he turned to account each passing event to teach a lesson to his disciples . . . the lessons they had to learn, if they were to bear fruit.

But Thursday quickly follows Sunday, especially when it is the last week of the holidays, as it were. What was there odd about the instruction to the two disciples with regard to preparing the Pasch? Simply that the man carrying a pitcher of water is not a common sight, even today, for it is the women who do the fetching and carrying. At any rate, nowadays the commemoration of the Passion, properly so called, begins near the scene of the Last Supper, on Mount Sion, outside the present walls of the city. Here the Franciscans hold a service; and immediately after, a hymn being sung, they all leave the chapel, and wind along the ragged path, down into the deep valley, and then climbing slightly, across the brook, they reach the cool, dappled darkness of Gethsemane. In recent years, a basilica has been built in the garden, a regular memorial to a unity of nations which nothing else can forge, for contributions came pouring in for its building from all parts of the world, new and old alike. It is modern, but in the centre of the nave, before the High Altar, the floor is formed of the living rock, at the spot traditionally assigned to the Agony of Christ, while outside, the calm moon looks down upon a garden of olives still, for they say the olive never dies. And here for one hour they watch with Christ, and do not many eyes grow heavy in that hour? Mine certainly did, but then I go to sleep at the slightest provocation, anywhere.

There was, however, no rest for our Lord that night. How sad we do not more often keep an all-night vigil before the Blessed Sacrament at the Altar of Repose on Maundy Thursday night. No, Christ was taken off to the High Priest, and the pilgrim can go the same way, finding a modern French church in the modern French style built upon the spot where they believe the house of Caiphas to have stood. There, cut deep into the rocks, are prison cells. Did Christ spend the night in one of these? Does it really matter? Why this ceaseless argument? The very truth of the whole Gospel story is borne in on your minds as you trudge coldly back into the city, for from the depth of the night, a cock crows. We are apt to think of this little incident as untoward. Not so at all; it was an everyday occurrence, even in the city; and for this very reason Jesus Christ used it, as he did other common objects, to teach Peter, and no only Peter but every future man, to feel his own individual denial of Christ, whenever a cock crows. We get out of touch with this, especially in a city, for we more often see a dead bedraggled chicken hanging head downwards in a poultry shop than hear a cock crow. But it was and is not so in Jerusalem; the cock and hen, the cow and goat are part of the household in the East. It is no more astonishing in Jerusalem to look out and find a cow living on a roof and chewing cud there, than it is to find the black Coptic priests from Ethiopia living on the roof of the Holy Sepulchre. Cocks live there too; and for reasons best known to themselves, they sometimes call at night, raucous and spasmodic, across the sleeping city.

So the night passes, and brings the awful emptiness of Good Friday, the day when the very emptiness of our churches shouts at us that we have killed the Son of God by our sins. The first journey of Christ that day was to Pilate, and so, whatever the critics say, the pilgrims go to Gabatha or Lithostrothos, the area of the Governor's palace. Well below the level of the present street, near the Ecce Homo arch, is the courtyard of Pilate, the scene of the Scourging; here they kneel on the old Roman paving; here too on the stones is carved the symbol of a crown; some say it was the Roman soldiers' ancient gambling game, the game of the crown. If it was, was this the rude image which first put the idea of crowning the king of the Jews into the heads of his guards, adding agony to agony? A hundred archaeologists have produced a double number of reasons for discrediting this belief, but one is often made to feel a weariness for disproving in this city which points a finger all the time at history. Simple faith, too, can move a mountain; argument can kill a love.

Of the Way of the Cross, what shall I say? Do you ever hear a good person saying, or do you ever feel yourself saying, "I cannot make the Stations of the Cross in public; it is so distracting." If you do, think sometimes that the first way of the Cross was the public way, the street. And what a street; again, it is not the same today, but it is not likely to have been much better or much more different in the days of Simon the Cyrenean. The rough, uneven cobbles are often jagged-edged, often slippery; the distance is not great, but much is uphill; a quarter of a mile—that is about all; yet it takes some twenty minutes to negotiate at a slow pace. For the way passes through the bazaar; here on the eve of the Pasch, all Jerusalem, and much of the rest of Palestine is pushing, haggling, whining; the streets themselves are narrow; on each side is a serried mass of shops, encroaching their booths on the already overcrowded way; there are shops of cobblers, of trinket-makers, stalls of unleavened bread, piles of vegetables, oranges and herbs, the grim carcasses of Paschal lambs; here a greasy man lazily stirs a sizzling pan of spiced meats; the air is filled with garlic and the tintinnabulation of harness.

Then, down the centre, swings an ass, the crowd jostles and swears, a tray of sweetmeats is overturned, and in a minute the street is blocked with figures, cries and blows. I used often to wonder how it was that our Lady could speak to Jesus, and Veronica wipe his face even, as he went along, surrounded by guards. Now I can understand; in the thronging thoroughfare, if you are flattened against the house walls or the shop fronts, you could still put out your hand and touch the person passing in the centre of the street. So, too, the falls, falls upon the cobbles, all slippery with water, dung or blood from slaughtered animals ... here in this country, in your parish church, wherever you make the Stations, when the person next to you hacks you on the shins, think that our Lord went through the hurly-burly of an Eastern crowd; if you are weary as you strap-hang going home, if you cannot bear the scent the other girl in the office uses, if any of these things, think of Christ's weariness, of Christ's thirst, of the stench of garlic, blood and filth that swirled into Christ's face as he fell. So too when the *Stabat Mater* is out of tune, it always is if I sing it, think of the discordant cry of the vendor, and the wail of a blind beggar.

Is there just a possibility that we are wrong if we always seek solitude for our prayer, when prayer has to be a public thing too, as Christ showed so well, carrying his Cross. ... "Daughters of Jerusalem, weep not for me, but for yourselves and for your children."

Of Calvary, I can say nothing; whether it is the rush and scurry of several different services, or the quiet peace of night time, there is a wonder about Calvary, which even the tawdry ornaments of the East cannot dispel. On Good Friday, it is the loneliest place in the world, because the world has deserted God, and so deserted itself, and plunged into nonsensical isolation. The real awfulness of what man can do weighs down upon you on Calvary, until it is almost unbearable.

But Calvary is incomplete without the Sepulchre. Failure is incomplete without triumph as its outcome. The Gospel would have been vain if there had been no Resurrection, and so, without a doubt, my selfish joy was full at that pale time before the dawn, the time of the holy women. All the streets are sleeping, except for the twitter of birds, and a few beggars crouched in the doorways. The Church of the Holy Sepulchre is dark, but lights glimmer from Calvary and from the Tomb; near the entrance to the tomb itself sits young Brother Francis; his face is not unlike that of his holy father, the poor man of Assisi, who so longed to convert the Holy Places to completely Catholic worship by the fire of his love; but now Brother Francis rests his dark shorn head upon his roughened hands, wearily, almost mechanically, he tells the beads, as he watches the Mass being celebrated again inside the Sepulchre; Holy Week has taxed him to the limit, young though he is; for since Wednesday he has only snatched three hours' sleep; yet he rises to make room, so that we too can kneel and catch the first glimpse of Easter as the newly consecrated host is raised by the priest over the stone slab of the sepulchre. *Resurrexit sicut dixit, alleluia.*

And then again, we have one more lesson to learn, a lesson we could each well take to heart. It is the lesson which they keep near Jerusalem on Easter Monday, it is the lesson of the breaking of bread in which the two disciples knew our

Lord, in which we know our Lord, in which, for the rest of time, our Lord unites his Mystical Body—the Church.

Early in the morning, the Sabbath day's journey is undertaken . . . the road to Emmaus; it is not a road; the country road of Ireland is better than this bullock track. From the last scattered houses of Jerusalem, you plunge straightway into the rocky countryside, where much of the corn falls on bad ground, though the rest is already "white for the harvest" at this time of year. Set high above the great coastal plain, the hills fall right away from Emmaus, leaving it perched in space; while sweeping down to the blue floor of the distant Mediterranean, all the land lies rich and green, dappled with splashes of poppy and the flare of the yellow mustard. The air is clear with the newness of the new dawn, with the clarity of the Resurrection. All is beauty, peace, the silence of the country which is always full of minute sounds. The tranquillity of the Risen Christ has touched Emmaus . . . it is summed up in the Mass, said among the foundations believed to be those of the house of Cleophas. The rising sun slants through the air, where birds already echo the alleluias of the liturgy. And this liturgy is made to live again, not only in the literal breaking of bread in the Sacrifice, but also in the ancient custom long established, by which the friars set forth a repast of wine or coffee and fresh rolls for all comers on this day, that they too may feel the fellowship of the Church in the breaking of bread.

That, then, is my mental picture of Palestine, living today even as in the days of Christ. It is personal and does not claim to be profound. But perhaps it will help someone to use the Bible and the liturgy as a more nourishing spiritual diet. The little snippets we get in the Epistle and Gospel at Mass should do no more than whet our appetites for further reading. Not everyone is blessed with the opportunity of following the scenes of our Lord's Passion and Death on the ground where it happened; but most people nowadays can read, and we can all think. Sometimes we think almost too deeply, getting our spiritual life lost in technicalities. Rather than this, we must look with the eyes of a child, look through doubts and queries to see Christ crucified. For all the Scriptures, culminating with the Evangelists, focus our attention upon the Cross. Even so today, all focuses upon the Mass. There is no deeper truth than this, none more real and necessary to our progress. We must, therefore, learn to share the sacrifice which took place outside the walls of old Jerusalem. There is no need to go to Palestine for that purpose. Go rather straight to your local church. Go to the altar. Go today.

XV

SHARING THE SACRIFICE

THE central act of the liturgy is the Mass. It is an act in two senses, that of something done, and that of drama in the highest order. But despite the amount written round it in recent years, the idea of being a spectator only still infects many, perhaps the majority, of lay men and women. The Mass remains a service which we attend, not a sacrifice which we offer. Some of this vagueness is due to the care necessary in separating the priest from the people, in that we say the priest alone has a priestly function, by ordination, while the people are in no way priests, even though they too share in the offering. This is inclined to cloud the part of the people, to obscure the public nature of the Mass. For the Mass is by nature public and social, whether it is said in the solitude of the Sahara by Charles de Foucauld or in the Piccadilly-Circus crowd of a London Midnight Mass. The priest offers sacrifice for the whole Church, for the living, for the dead. This note is the most resounding of any in the liturgy, because the echo of each Mass has its effect upon each living person, more especially on each member of the Mystical Body. You do not feel any better for the Mass being offered now in the Philippines? Well, you are better, anyhow! What a joy it is, or should be, to belong to that body which, "from the rising of the sun to the going down thereof," is making God's name great among the Gentiles. Greater joy still to realize that we can take on the rôle of sponsors and workers in the offering, "doers of the word, not hearers only."

But the question at issue is how we are to persuade our

slow minds and hearts to take a more active part. Such phrases ring true and meaningless from school-desk to death-bed: "We are redeemed by his Precious Blood," "From the Mass flows every grace," "Christ our Pasch is sacrificed;" they roll off an idle tongue, learnt by rote, from a forgotten age of Catechism. Do they vitalize us, goad us to action? Do they draw us to Mass? To be frank: they do not. From a prayer book, from a preacher's tongue, they yawn with our bored yawn, waiting like us to get-on-with-the-job. A slow priest, we can get in ten minutes late; a quick priest, we can get out ten minutes early; meet me at the twelve-thirty Mass; the last Mass is at twelve, you say? Oh, but the sermon ends at half-past, that's when we always come along!

Sometimes we understand that to come to Mass is the greatest thing we can do in our lives. We even grasp the power now and then: how it achieves more than endless organizing, wins sinners back, converts pagans—yes, but now it is over, let's *do* something practical! Silly fools: that is all we are. Our only practical method should be to get up earlier, come to Mass more frequently, attend with greater interest and awe. Such action changes our lives, fills us full of the Holy Ghost, makes us sources of God's power over men. The miracle of conversion begins in us from the miracle of Calvary renewed and blossoms in the "daily miracle of a saintly life".

In some way or other we must find the incentive to wake up at Mass. It needs a bit to go out on a wet morning; it often needs more to change the breakfast routine, cutting out the relax-with-cigarette-and-paper period. Most people find it necessary to have a greater understanding in order to have greater appreciation. Some gain the required deepening through prayer alone, but being made with a mind, gener-ally it needs food for thought before the heart is moved at all. Without hesitation, then, I would say that everyone should read a book about the Mass. If the Catechism is the end of our development, we all know the young mind scarcely grasps, let alone appreciates, spiritual values behind exam-worn definitions. Lack of knowledge breeds lack of interest, which mixes with stronger worldly attractions to create perfunctory attendance at the last Mass, whittling down to complete collapse. But what to read? Try Mgr. Knox's *Mass in Slow Motion*. Why? Because he was talking to children, trying to liven their interest, which is just what we need. There are innumerable other books, of course; you must suit your taste. Some will like Frs. Coventry and Gillick's *The Breaking of Bread*, an interesting explanation with beautiful illustrations; more spiritual is Zundel's lovely *The Splendour of the Liturgy*, while the studious will gain a new angle of value in theological approaches from de la Taille, Masure and Billot. The only important thing is to probe into these books until you find a flash of understanding into the magnetism of the Mass.

It goes without saying that reading alone would be lopsided and absurd. We can go so far as to say knowledge is of less need than practice; as is the case with all prayer, practice makes perfect. The accent, though, is not only on attendance bodily, but on dynamic spiritual co-operation. A wordy, meaningless sentence? No. We are not told to come to church to find a method of whiling away the time from the first dab of holy water to the Last Gospel. Pius XII states that the faithful may say the Rosary during the liturgy, as not all can cope with the missal, whereas the "Hail Mary" and thoughts on the life of our Lord are in keeping with the spirit that liturgy is proclaiming. Nevertheless, such a practice is not a dope to fill up an idle half-hour: it is to be a stimulant to our understanding of the sacrifice. By this or other means, we are to realize the full share in offering which we, as individual Christians, make. Be quite clear; this is not the priestly power, which is given only in ordination; this is a real and effective participation in the offering belonging to each layman, a participation which varies with the earnestness of the person present. To sit and wonder why Mrs Upright uses the shade of lipstick which clashes with her Sunday hat is to miss our share in the offering; to become suddenly absorbed in the Table of Movable Feasts (I wonder how many Sundays there are after Pentecost this year, anyhow?) may mean missing that bit when the priest says, "Pray, brethren, that my sacrifice and yours may be acceptable to God the Father Almighty".... When he says what? Well, that is the English for *Orate Fratres*, you know. But what sacrifice of mine? That was the one you should have been offering when the priest offered the host and chalice; that was your chance to begin offering yourself, your life, your friends, your worries, your joys ... well, of course, you were looking for that sixpence for the plate; so annoying of it to get lost!

Much of the difficulty is that it is so easy to drift through Mass. For that reason, it would be a good thing to fix a series of hooks to hang your attention on. Do you not think, as an example, that it is tremendously easy even to miss the Sign of the Cross at the beginning, especially when the priest mumbles it? Before you know where you are, he is up the altar steps and away, leaving you still trying to discover if it is the twelfth or thirteenth after Whitsun. It would be a good plan to decide at least to get the first sign in with the priest; it checks you on being late, too! Think if everyone in church did that together, a united, terrifying act of resolve to focus ourselves on this Mass as a living sacrifice, not only God's drama, but our own.

After that, the intention must carry on. The first part, to the end of the Creed, is instructional; it is there that we can gain knowledge—"cud to chew over during the day," as it were. I begin the day depressed, then the opening psalm asks: "Why

art thou cast down, O my soul? . . . Hope thou in God."
Kyrie eleison, Lord have mercy on me in temptation, Christ
have mercy on me in my pride of success, my depression of
failure. Because now at the *Gloria* I know why I am alive. . . .
"We praise thee, we adore thee, we glorify thee," however
odd the way may seem. What, the Epistle already? where is
the lesson here? A "Confessor not a Bishop" (How do you
pronounce that word Confessor? I am always shifting the
accent from first to second and back again); anyhow, it tells
us to be fools for Christ's sake, fools in kneeling here, fools in
wasting time which might be spent in bed, fools in not being
out in the country relaxing; but no! the Gospel shouts, for
where your treasure is, there is your heart also. That's what
we came for, to put our hearts on the altar, by sacrificing our
wills with Christ. But where is my heart . . . wandering home
to breakfast? Steady now, we are not through yet.

With the Gospel over we really get down to the Mass. No.
I do not mean down on the bench to take it easy. I mean the
sacrifice proper begins here, from the Offertory to the Communion. Just to emphasize that this is not the place to sit back
and let the priest do the work alone, digest these words of
Pope Pius XII on the people's part: "It means they must
assume to some extent the character of a victim, that they
deny themselves as the Gospel commands, that freely and of
their own accord they do penance, and that each detests and
satisfies for his sins. It means, in a word, that we must all
undergo with Christ a mystical death on the Cross, so that
we can apply to ourselves the words of St Paul: 'With Christ
I am nailed to the Cross.' "

That passage is strong! If we could let it penetrate our
minds and hearts as we kneel at the bench in shifty dreari-
ness we should have a greater share in "filling up what is
wanting in the sufferings of Christ". After the Preface, except
for bells ringing, we are left to drift or to follow silently.

Silence most deeply expresses love; silence is most profound prayer; silence unites us closely to the intentions of the Church, to the prayer of Christ, to the sacrifice of the priest. The silent hymn of the liturgy throbs between High Priest, priest and people, as the priest says: *Memento Domine* ... "Be mindful, Lord, of thy servants and handmaids ... for whom we offer or who offer up to thee this sacrifice of praise for themselves and theirs, for the redemption of their souls. . . ."

How many of us, in fact, make the offering with the priest? If we do make it verbally, is it true of us that "out of the full-ness of the heart, the mouth speaketh"? For the offering verbally with the priest is not enough. Somehow we must follow St Paul: "I beseech you therefore ... that you present your bodies, a living sacrifice, holy, pleasing unto God." Because here we come upon an amazing paradox, most startling in the case of the priest, but nearly as amazing for those who share in the Mass. It is this. The Mass, infinite in value, perfect, complete and unchangeable in itself, never-theless is made more perfect, is more complete, is of more value extrinsically, in so far as a holy priest is celebrating worthily, and in so far as those in the congregation are holy, are full of fervour, are uniting with High Priest and priest to offer themselves as a spiritual sacrifice. Astounding? It is the paradox of God's bounty to man, that God allows man to co-operate in or to limit his work. God's greatest gift to man, freedom, thus becomes the binding or loosing force for the graces God plans to shower upon us. If we can feel this pulse of man's co-operation beating through God's plan, it will lead us to redouble our efforts, lest we frustrate his plan. Each time we doze or yawn through Mass, that Mass is so much the less effective; each time we take our part fully, those merits of the Precious Blood abound the more in this world which today so lacks grace. Here indeed is the centre of

Catholic Action, Catholic and active to a greater extent than any other because of its universal application and infinite power. Moreover, we fulfil literally: "If any man will come after me. . . ."

There is another doctrine which gives even more striking proof of our instrumentality in the Mass. A horrid word, that, but expressive of our sharing in the sacrifice by accepting all that is implied when Christ said: "Abide in me, and I in you." St Paul saw the point, cried out: "I live, now not I, but Christ liveth in me." We all know the awful consequences to a person "possessed by the devil"; he is no longer master of his actions. Equally radical, though totally different, the possession by Christ, if we allow it. How shall we relate it to our action at Mass? What effect will it have?

The answer is simple. Christ in us breaks down our personal, centralized approach; it is no bore, but something we watch, not something beyond our grasp. For self must be put aside, while Christ acts in us, sacrifices in us. He is the driving force, we are humble co-operators. Christ directly in and through the priest at the altar is sacrificing again. We in the congregation, surrendered, drawing life as members of the Body, can only co-operate in so far as Christ, living in us, has taken command. Always in accord with our willing surrender, he makes use of our willing lips to adore, praise, thank and beg his Father; loving Son giving supreme joy to his Father, he uses the Father's most perfect creatures as instruments of worship.

Unless an instrument does the work intended by the workman, it fails in its purpose. As channels of Christ's prayer we must, then, take on his attitude to the Cross. What would this be? The dreamy unawareness which clouds the eyes and mind at Mass? Weariness perhaps, for surely he was weary on Calvary, but a weariness livened by whole-hearted giving. Just at such a time of inability are we most empty, most ready "to become as like as possible to Christ in his most grievous sufferings" by which "he emptied himself, becoming obedient unto death, even the death of the Cross". We do not lack emptiness, we lack emptying. All our personal feelings crowd into our empty heads . . . how stuffy it is; the priest dawdles; that airman is chewing gum again; why do Italians eat garlic? Why all this discomfort?—at least pad the kneelers! Why the Mass? Because of the suffering of the Cross? Well, why the Cross then . . . ? It was just for this that he emptied himself. Only the hardest death, most cruel suffering could be an example to us; only by hanging three hours on the tree could he persuade us to kneel for thirty minutes. Do we recognize the lead, as the Body of Christ is raised again above the altar? "My Lord and my God" . . . an answer to his appeal from our hearts, or just "Hullo, do get on with it; we are missing the bus"? What a lot besides buses we miss, our minds chasing shadows, conscious or unconscious. To God or Mammon for one half-hour. . . . To let, one semi-detached mind and heart!

Here, as elsewhere, Christ our model leads us to Calvary, living now and again upon every altar in the Church. To come at all is something, but only part. The soldiers came on that first Good Friday . . . to crucify. Shall we, like them, sit scoffing, gossiping, passing the time, waiting to breathe a sigh of relief at the end, when we can get on with living? If we do this, we are failing him indeed. He alone on the Cross, we with the choice of being the "beloved disciple" or the un-moved soldiery. Pope Pius XII continually urges the better part upon us: "Now the exhortation of the Apostle: 'Let this mind be in you which was also in Christ Jesus', requires that all Christians should possess, as far as is humanly possible, the same dispositions as those which the divine Redeemer had when he offered himself in sacrifice: that is to say they should in a humble attitude of mind pay adoration, honour, praise and thanksgiving to the supreme Majesty of God." Quite a big task, as we sit there dumbly. Yet the *Pater Noster*, coming in the centre of the most solemn part, should rouse us outwardly and inwardly. I always like the idea they have abroad of ringing the bell just before the *Pater Noster*. We have reached such an important point. The priest with all the people is talking to God the Father in the words Christ taught his apostles. Even supposing we could say we were lost in the rest of the Mass, we cannot say so here. "Our Father." How many say it with the priest? If we do, we "pay adoration, honour, praise and thanksgiving to the supreme Majesty of God". Christ speaks through the priest to his Father in the acts of faith, hope and charity which make up the first section of the prayer. He speaks through each member of the congregation, in so far as "this mind be in you which was in Christ Jesus. . . ." Oh dear, I wish I wasn't always so dozy; he's slipped on to the *Agnus Dei*, and I didn't even make the sign of the Cross at the *fractio*, when the body of our Lord is symbolically reunited in a new Resurrection. Strange, really, how that custom is dying; it seems to belong to the era of Bishop Challoner. Who made the first sign of the Cross, anyhow? That may have been the way our Lord blessed his apostles before he ascended into heaven. Which reminds me again that it is the Mass, and time to go up to Communion, the consummation of the sacrifice just as the Ascension was: God the Father receiving the Son in glory, we receiving the Son, our "pledge of future glory".

We may be inclined to forget too easily the importance of our Communion. For the priest, it is an essential part of the Mass, which may not be omitted, because without it the sacrifice is incomplete. Though not essential to the people attending Mass, it is clear that the union in offering will be much greater if we receive the body of our Lord. The hard years of Jansenism must be cut out from our spirituality.

How they cling! It is the God of love who urges us to partake. From a personal point of view, this act is also one of the best hooks upon which to hang the wandering strands of our attention. And even supposing that for some good reason sacramental Communion is impossible all the same, a spiritual Communion is always possible.

Yet here again, just because of the tremendous thing which is happening to us and in us, we even find the greatest difficulty in keeping awake. Innumerable very holy people, saints too, have exclaimed how hard it is to concentrate at this moment. Everything is distractingly dry, lonely, dark, blank, muddled; the only clear thought runs down alleyways, plays games, is tempted. Our desires for God, love, thanks, delight—poor smothered things—get no chance. It may be battle royal to believe. Then we can help ourselves only by letting God help us. Eating the body of Christ, we should force to our lips, if force is necessary, an act of love at that very moment. Afterwards, we must lean gently on love, making the love of God one with our love, that we may take into ourselves, not the body only, but also the Spirit of Christ. It is within us that Christ wills to continue his life; Christ lives in us for this short time, not only Spirit, but body also. Oh, there we go—another yawn, a pity Father is so slow, we'll never get breakfast and catch the ten o'clock; what, another collection?—what for this time? Lord, do you believe in all these collections? Is paying the best form of praying for me? I can't seem to do both at once, but anyhow that is all I've got—threepence—it won't redecorate the Sanctuary, but it may help to keep the lamp alight in my heart.

Ite Missa est—that *Deo gratias* comes out a bit too slickly. Thank God it is over! Perhaps one day, Lord, you will manage to change our tune, if we keep coming to let out our hearts to you. Then, too, we may understand more that a

perfunctory bob in the Last Gospel isn't good enough, because, believing, we are made the sons of God, and so we
know that the Word made flesh dwelt, and literally dwells,
among and in us.

XVI

THE EXAMPLE OF PADRE PIO

As an example of the living liturgy and sacramental life there is in modern times an extraordinary case with Padre Pio of Pietrelcina. Something has been heard of him in recent years in England, though not all is satisfactory or correct. To include a descriptive account of him here is not entirely out of place, if he is seen as a possible signpost in God's plan, pointing the way of Christian life back to the essentials of prayer and sacrifice, especially in the Mass. While he lives, no full account of him can be given, but an impression may help to deepen our spiritual lives. In this and any similar cases, however, we must take great care to avoid hysteria and the seeking of odd physical phenomena, as these are by no means part of our life with God. We are expected to live by faith, assisted at each step, according to the bequest of Christ to his Church, by receiving grace sufficient for our needs through the Sacraments.

Early in the morning, before five, the sacristy door at St Giovanni Rotondo, near Foggia, opens and Padre Pio comes in to say Mass. He comes in slowly, almost shuffling. A tired face, the beard tinged with grey; a large nose, slightly splayed-out from snuff-taking; eyes that pierce and laugh, while the mouth and cheeks follow the eyes; a face serene, radiant, simple. Quite stout, quite short—you see such figures every day on the roads of Italian towns and country-side—the Cappucini.

From that moment the day goes quickly. The main purpose of this priest's life is the main purpose of the life of every priest—the Mass. It is an act of worship; here it lasts an hour and a half, but it is not a performance. In anticipation it was one of the things about which to be sceptical. Not so in reality. For the rest of the day he is in and out of the confessional; he prays quietly in the choir; he gives answers to questions received in letters; he has one meal only, at midday, eating with the rest of the community, and in the evening he joins them at recreation. Monotonous, wearying, unspectacular; it is all these things. Let us look more closely then at various aspects and their effects.

There has been considerable research and reporting in recent times upon the origin of the phenomenon called stigmatism, or the appearance of wounds upon a person's hands, feet and side, usually connected with those borne upon our Lord's body at the Crucifixion. The general medical opinion today seems to be that hysteria probably cannot produce wounds like stigmata spontaneously, though the question remains open. It is considered, however, that the world of fantasy in which the hysteric lives is such that he or she may inflict the wounds, without seeing anything fraudulent or wrong in the act. If hysteria can be excluded and the general life indicates sanctity, the Church admits the possibility of a supernatural origin. But care is most necessary, and no direct acknowledgement is given during the lifetime of the person concerned. At all times, apart from the "victim" the Church must safeguard her children from false mystics, and even in the case of the true mystic, from becoming hysterical themselves, losing their way to heaven by chasing unnecessary phenomena and miracles. Thus very great caution, even placing a ban upon public activity, may result after remarkable events. At the most, tacit approval is given, while a vigilant guard is kept to stamp out "canonization" and hysteria among the faithful.

Padre Pio received the marks of our Lord's wounds in the

year 1915, while he was staying at his home near Benevento. He was in the garden, and he received them invisibly, the only indication, later recalled by his mother, being a waving of the hand, as though in pain, when he came in to his meal. He passed this off as nothing, and no more was said. In 1918 he received the wounds visibly, while making his thanksgiving in the choir at S. Giovanni Rotondo. He has remained ever since an ordinary friar, living there in a small and poor community of about twenty. From his ordination in 1910 he had been outstanding as a priest, not particularly because he was brilliant intellectually, but because he possessed that something which draws the faithful to the confessional and the Sacraments. This something the ordinary people recognize. They sum it up differently as different aspects strike them—gentleness, understanding, humility, goodness, charity, or simply holiness. From his ordination he took an unusually long time to say Mass.

As soon as the stigmatization was known to have happened, he was "canonized" locally, even more than before. This was a proof of what they had understood all along. But Padre Pio's superiors and later Rome kept a careful check upon his activities. Interest and veneration grew to hysteria. The reaction in official circles was to prohibit the public appearance of Padre Pio for a period of about two years, during which time he was forbidden to say Mass in public or to hear confessions. Meanwhile, intensive examination of the wounds was carried out and attempts made to heal them. Padre Pio submitted to all questioning, examination and medical attention, from the external methods of healing to diets. He was entirely obedient to his superiors, though the separation from his outward work for souls was a trial to him. Subsequently he was allowed to resume public saying of Mass and hearing confessions. Certain strict rules were imposed, and Rome still keeps watch to see there are no irregularities.

Now, although the natural thought at first for many visitors is to see the stigmata, this is soon dwarfed by a deeper attraction—a spiritual power sensed rather than seen. No one, in fact, has much chance to see the wounds. Padre Pio's hands are covered with woollen mittens at all times. The only exception is during Mass, when the sleeves of the alb, purposely long, reach down to the fingers, only accidentally falling back far enough for those nearby to see the scarred palms at *Dominus Vobiscum* or the blessing. When, walking from the sacristy to the confessional, people seize his hands, touching, pulling, squeezing, he has sometimes to raise them above his head, remonstrating. He is walking with a purpose: he is a Capuchin; he is a priest doing his "father's business", he is not a peepshow. So he turns sharply on those who jostle and talk in front of the Blessed Sacrament; he tells people plainly to reverence God and not to behave as though they were at a market. Once asked, "Do the stigmata hurt you?" he replied simply, "Do you think God gave them to me as an ornament?"

The impression is not that he desires publicity, but that he bears it; he accepts what amounts to a daily persecution because it is the means given to draw men to God. Thus, there are no particular ecstasies on Feast Days or Fridays; there is seldom noticeable bleeding from the wounds; nothing is visible when he walks about to mark him off from any other friar. Moreover, the stigmata are no excuse for being idle. Padre Pio does more than a full day's work. He is seldom ill. His health had improved since he was pensioned from the army on account of sickness. In fact, each day more people come to him than he can see; he spends long hours in the confessional; he is given not a moment of peace while he is in public; each morning he faces a battery of requests, monotonous, unchanging year in, year out. Given a little understanding, a watcher must find springing to his mind that this is enough "to try the patience of a saint".

To sum up: the half a dozen or more times I have stayed at S. Giovanni Rotondo have impressed upon me the merely secondary importance of the stigmata. In fact, the theoretical teaching of mystical theologians here has outward expression. Beyond the phenomenon, one is drawn by the Christlikeness of Padre Pio. This leads men to want to follow his example, not physically, but in his whole life, echoing St Paul's "with Christ I am nailed to the Cross". The open wounds are not necessary for the nailing, they are only there displayed, as it were, after the nailing of complete surrender has taken place. With us, unfortunately, it has scarcely begun, as we admit to ourselves when we examine our consciences. Padre Pio's generosity in giving himself without reservation is sealed by the imprint. But the giving came first; the phenomenon followed as an "unnecessary" gift from God. And now any-one in conversation with this friar is taken back, again and again, behind the phenomenon itself to the deep mystery of God's love expressed in suffering upon the Cross.

From what has been said, it will be clear that Padre Pio is quite simply fulfilling the purpose of the priesthood, to be *Alter Christus*. Now, more intensely than at any other time, the priest stands for Christ when he stands at the altar for Mass. And here, too, Padre Pio focuses attention on to the Sacrifice. When he says an ordinary Low Mass, it lasts for about ninety minutes, excluding any giving of Communion. That is unquestionably overstepping the rubrics and is a point liable to raise objections and to cause scandal. How-ever, it has occurred not infrequently in the history of the Church, with such a matter of fact person as St Ignatius of Loyola and with St Philip Neri, to quote two examples only.

There is all the difference between a very slow priest saying Mass normally, and this Capuchin. To say that assisting at Mass offered by Padre Pio is a greater spiritual benefit than a week in retreat is merely a way of describing what I mean.

It has often resulted in something far deeper than devotion; it has brought a complete change of heart, a beginning of faith from atheism. It would be useless to describe an action which must be witnessed. Suffice it to say that there is nothing really extraordinary, no levitations, blood from the wounds in great quantities or marked ecstasies. The most penetrating thing is the absolute surrender of the priest, who has put on the Lord Jesus. Suffering is manifest, but not picturesque; the intensity draws the average person to realize, perhaps for the first time, that the Mass is a real sacrifice, not a distant reproduction; that the priest offers and shares with the victim. To stand or kneel during this Mass in garlic-laden air, hemmed in, feeling faint, fighting to concentrate, all this makes the penance a good one for the congregation. It is a test of faith, and an act of love. Surprisingly, when the end comes, the time has gone with extreme rapidity. Does the length drive people away as it would in the normal course of events? On the contrary, they come in ever increasing numbers to crowd round the altar and share the sacrifice.

It is not necessary to go to S. Giovanni Rotondo to learn the meaning of the Mass more deeply. It can be done before any altar. But at S. Giovanni you will see what it means to say "I preach Christ and him Crucified". For that reason it can also be a stumbling block. To a priest, however—and I have spoken to many who have been there—comes a deeper and more lasting insight into the way his daily Mass can and should transform him; that through him, Christ may transform the world. To a lay person, here is a living example which has the effect of increasing his love for the Sacrifice by helping him to appreciate how active a sacrifice it should be for the priest and people. Hence it seems a manifest expression of Christ's prophecy: "I, if I be lifted up from the earth, will draw all men to me."

The priest has one endless duty—to get his charges to the Sacraments. After his Mass and thanksgiving, Padre Pio goes to the confessional. It is quite a new experience for an English woman to be told that as there are so many other women in front of her, her turn to go to Confession will not come for two or three days. Yet women waiting to confess to Padre Pio must first stand in a queue to book a place in the queue, and later queue for the confession itself. Men are more fortunate, as they generally manage to be shriven during the first or second day, except at Eastertide, when the situation becomes impossible. Strange tales are told of people sent away before confession as impenitent, of others whose secret sins have been revealed to them when not immediately confessed, of communist apostates reconciled, of lives directed anew without prior human knowledge. These are true for the most part, the witness to truth being the testimony of those restored to faith who now spend their days in work, prayer and penance.

To my mind, however, a far more wonderful manifestation of the supernatural is in the unceasing succession of plain, ordinary penitents who have committed all the usual sins, nothing very terrible, have done nothing wonderfully good, the peasants, with their beads, the better-dressed men and women from the towns, the varying classes and peoples who are indeed the little people of God's kingdom. They come with faith for comfort, for counsel, for guidance, above all for the forgiveness of God. The stream is continuous for several hours a day for seven days a week. Any priest who has sat at all long in a confessional will recognize the patience, gentleness and understanding necessary for this task. It is interesting to watch Padre Pio from a distance in the sacristy as he shrives the men. He seems now to chide, now to soothe, now to joke, now to emphazise a point. He is not slow to send away trouble-makers, or to speak out in no uncertain terms if he sees someone trying to get ahead of the queue. And invariably he keeps to the rule, leaving the confessional in time for the community meal or recreation. It is all so simple, with no idea of the extraordinary. Yet even the most common-place confession brings sureness and consolation, which cannot be traced, perhaps, to a particular word spoken or to a gesture; it seems the natural outpouring of God's grace through the priestly channel. "Come to me, all ye that labour and are heavy burdened" . . . it applies to every priest in every confessional, but we all know that some aid us more than others, and Padre Pio appears as one of these. Penance brings pardon, and pardon peace. In the sacristy and confessional at S. Giovanni Rotondo, *pax et bonum* prevail not more truly than elsewhere (the Sacrament is the same), but more cogently perhaps because expressed by one to whom might be applied "Now not I, but Christ liveth in me".

For several hours each day and for the whole night, Padre Pio is within the enclosure. That is not strange when it is considered that as a member of a community he is bound to obedience to attend the community exercises. These are to some extent modified in his case by the decision of his superiors to allow extra time for hearing confessions. He also eats very little, having only one meal a day, but this he has with the other friars. What is immediately noticeable is the continuation of the ordinary life of the community, as it were, in spite of Padre Pio. Special arrangements have to be made for his Mass, but while it is going on, the other friars are saying public Masses, giving Communion and saying their Office in choir. October devotions, sermons, Benedictions go on according to schedule.

Inside the convent there is peace, broken into by the continual clang of the enclosure bell or the loud talking of the crowds, but nevertheless peace. For the porter, for superiors, for the friars themselves, there must be many trials, many annoyances connected with living in this atmosphere of pilgrimage. Yet the attachment to and affection for Padre Pio is genuine and strong in the community. One of the most enlightening experiences is not open to many. This is to go into the garden on a summer evening during recreation. There, under the vines and among the cypresses, the Padre enjoys an hour or so of relaxation with those of the friars who are not busy and a few friends (one might say disciples), members of the Third Order. He is completely relaxed, the soul of the party. His interests are wide, ranging through politics and contemporary events to the number of Italians in London, his experiences in the army, the English cult of pets, the crops, the cost of living. He argues and is contradicted, he chaffs those sitting by, he takes snuff, passes it round, listens with interest to news and stories, is quick with repartee, has a lively sense of humour. Here I found a Gospel atmosphere, thinking again and again of the disciples clustered round our Lord, questioning him, doubting his opinions, and not slow to voice their own, in no way quelled by magnificence but rather encouraged to talk by the humility and ready understanding of the listener.

His whole attitude to life and to people is summed up again yet undefinably, as holiness. The effect is to radiate peace and joy; his face is alight: being with Padre Pio you can catch the eager begging of the apostles in the "Lord, teach us to pray". His fellow friars come by and pause to joke gaily; he is rebuked for having no faith in doctors; yet he is recollected in his lightheartedness. There is something about those evenings under the vines which lingers with you long afterwards, which perhaps does not die. But like all human things, there is an end, for the community has a bell and a routine, so Padre Pio says good-night in the corridor with a smile, a blessing and a characteristic cuff on the side of the head with his mittened hand.

From peace, the visitor is ejected to a world of noise. The

cramped *ristorante* where he goes to eat is overflowing with pilgrims, many of whom have been several times before and are proclaiming all they have seen and heard of Padre Pio to the less initiated. There is a true foundation for a great part of what is said. It is an objective fact that there is a perfume which fills the air at intervals and has an odour unknown to the world. There are well authenticated stories of healing, well checked evidence of bilocation; these and many others are spread by the ardent pilgrims, who probably embroider them unwittingly. When new pilgrims arrive late at night they find all this; people captivated, people rebuffed, people disconsolate at missing confession owing to the crowd, but all with one mind determining to come again when possible.

Miracles are not for discussion here. But one thing must be said. Padre Pio has never publicly prophesied anything, either war, earthquakes or the end of the world. Nor does he heal publicly at S. Giovanni, though sick are brought to him. Bodily miracles attributed to him are worked at a distance from the convent which he himself is forbidden to leave under obedience. As with Christ, the cure of the soul has priority. Here is the sane and healthy fact which goes so far to support the nature of his spirituality. Nothing could be further from hysteria, to all appearances, than this humble friar's behaviour. For naturalness and humility work together with him. Whether he is taking snuff, ordering the women to stop gossiping in church, or joking with the community, there is nothing affected. You have only to see him to grasp his deep humility. It is difficult to explain, it has to be experienced. Hemmed in by special regulations on one side, by a crowd which is often rude and thoughtless on the other, tormented by questions, pestered for blessings, cures, advice— nevertheless he continues unaffectedly to do his work as a priest, saying Mass, hearing confessions, giving counsel. To see him, you would never imagine his daily stack of letters amounted to four hundred, or that he was visited by bishops, priests and people from all over the world. Meekness and humility, his *Domine non sum dignus* said with his eyes and heart fixed on God echoes back another act of humility: "I can do all things in him who strengtheneth me."

If this account is over-coloured, it does not contain a measure of the spiritual effect that flows from S. Giovanni Rotondo. But converts are often over-enthusiastic in the eyes of their more staid companions in the faith, and I was, as it were, converted to belief in Padre Pio. This came about by visiting him, because he crystallizes what I had been taught, what I had been trying and still am trying to learn of the spiritual life. He emphasizes continually and above all other considerations the primary importance of holiness, especially in a priest. To this end he focuses everything into love, shown by complete emptying of self in the service of love, through absolute humility and obedience. This he expresses in the Sacrifice of the Mass, carried on throughout the day in total surrender to God's children. I am not a doctor of psychology or mystical theology, but to me the actual phenomenon of the stigmata seems unconnected with hysteria, and in any case of minor importance except in so far as it appears to mark previous and continued conformity to the will of God. Finally, if there is any truth in our Lord's words "by their fruits you shall know them", then Padre Pio's influence would seem to come under the category of good fruit, for it has already happened many times that

> *Truth from his lips prevailed with double sway*
> *And fools, who came to scoff, remained to pray.*[1]

[1] Oliver Goldsmith, ' The Deserted Village '.

XVII

THE BEGINNING AND THE END

"THE ideal of Christian life," says Pope Pius XII in his Encyclical *Mediator Dei*, "is the close and uninterrupted union of everyone with God."

Everyone!

The Pope is the shepherd and teacher of us all, and his statement to us all does no more than echo the words of Christ, whom we are to follow as Christians—"Be ye perfect as your heavenly Father is perfect." The Holy Father goes on to explain how the life of the Church caters for just this ideal: "Therefore the worship which the Church pays to Almighty God, and which is founded mainly upon the Eucharistic Sacrifice and the use of the Sacraments, is so arranged that by means of the Divine Office it takes within its scope every hour of the day, every week, and the whole course of the year, all the seasons and all the various phases of human life.

"The divine Master commanded his disciples that 'they ought to pray continually, and never be discouraged'."[1]

The point of emphasis, then, is the all-embracing nature of the quest for God. Not only does it take in the whole life of one particular section of the community, but of all mankind, and beyond that the whole life of the whole of creation. Man by his very nature as the crown of this creation cannot cut himself adrift from the reality of creation's purpose, shown so clearly by the Psalmist:

> *Give praise to the Lord on earth, monsters of the sea and all its depth;*

[1] C.T.S. translation, Part II, p. 57

*Fire and hail, snow and mist, and the storm wind that executes his
    decree;*
All you mountains and hills, all you fruit trees and cedars;
*All you wild beasts and cattle, creeping things and birds that fly in
    the air;*
*All you kings and peoples of the world, all you that are princes and
    judges on earth;*
*Young men and maids, old men and boys together; let them all give
    praise to the Lord's name.*
*His name is exalted as no other, his praise reaches beyond heaven
    and earth;*
*And now he has given fresh strength to his people. Shall not his
    faithful servants praise him . . . ?*[1]

No one has any right to say that he is not included—"This
is not for me" leads only to disillusion and unhappiness.

Prayer, steps to heaven, the deepening of the spiritual life,
all these are open to you with the openness of God. The
liturgy is the book of life to be read and loved and lived by all,
whether God calls man or woman to the cloister or the hearth.
The Mass is a public sacrifice which must be shared by all the
people with the priest, even though they cannot usurp his
unique sacrificial office.

All the outlines that have gone before, ideas on prayer,
feeble efforts to enliven the seasons of the liturgy, the actual
example given of a living priest, seemingly closely united to
God, all this pointing is at you, that you may feel the necessity
of doing something more about it yourself.

First you must look round at the ideal of man as quoted
above; then see how far short the average falls. But, be more
particular than this. See how far short *you* fall.

Next, determine what is to be done.

I spoke earlier of giving one hour a day to God, or at least
fifteen minutes. This is not very much, if you love God and

---

[1] Ps. 148 (Knox translation).

believe your whole life to centre upon him. But here and now it is necessary to be eminently practical, cutting your coat to the measure of your cloth. In other words, the theory of being a saint, the theory of giving this time to God, has to be translated into act in your daily round. It is better, therefore, to begin with a minimum, that you may be quite sure of living up to it; otherwise a grand, but top-heavy, plan may collapse under the first strain. The minimum must be maintained day in, day out, for fifty-two weeks in the year.

If then, still aiming at the ideal, I demand from you ten minutes' prayer a day, do not immediately say that this is nothing at all. Do not be offended at the suggestion and say it is not worth while.

It is intensely worth while!

Why, there are many people, ourselves often included, who cannot find time even for a single syllable of love of God, let alone ten minutes. Now, you cannot worthily give less than ten minutes. Make up your mind to give it daily. Nothing at all must prevent this; sickness, worry, social engagements, business, the family ties at home are all included in your life, but do not exclude this ten minutes, ever. It is for this very reason that it is safer not to declare immediately for half an hour of meditation. It might work, but there are those days, long and tiring, when we want only to flop into bed at the end, and prayer has not been completed. Ten minutes then can seem an eternity, half an hour an impossibility.

No, be practical. Start low and work up. The time may come, you may be at it already, when you can go to Mass each morning and meditate for half an hour as well. Thank God if that is so; do not be discouraged if it is not. Certainly, by beginning on a small scale with no set rules as to how to pray, these will grow from your regularity and faithfulness, and if sown rightly, the seed will wish to swell from ten minutes also.

The way to encourage growth is without doubt to put the emphasis upon Mass and Communion. Should anyone try to go every day? That is the ideal, yet again it is necessary to be practical. Much better decide to go once or twice in the week, and to stick to that, than to begin with a rush and end with an extra half hour in bed.

Again and again it must be re-stated that perhaps the majority of people could get to Mass during the week. Perhaps the majority do not even let the idea cross the mind. It needs discipline and resolution. Sunday is only one day in the week. Mass is said on seven days, God is keeping you alive on seven days. Where is the sacrifice? Ah, breakfast! Yes, a daily occupation, needing adjustment to fit Mass or Communion or both. Is that adjustment impossible? By no means. Earlier to bed, earlier to rise. God *must* come first.

Think this over most earnestly as a challenge. You yourself, your family, your friends, the world as a whole stand in desperate need of more prayer, more spirituality. But that means willingness to show love of God and one's neighbour. It means cutting down on your own selfishness in order to give more to God. The way is certainly open to all—it is strange that mankind is not ashamed at its lack of generosity in responding. Sorrow, suffering and death itself are all noble and worth while if understood in terms of the love of God. All men can understand if the effort is made whole heartedly.

There can be no better example of the way God can work upon human material in a short time than this following story of an Irish boy of fifteen and a half who died recently of cancer. He was living in a London slum, as his father had left his mother. While he was himself in hospital, his mother died of cancer. He had already lost one leg with the disease, but was full of the will to live. He was scared of death, resentful of being ill, keen to get back to the cinema, T.V., his friends round the corner. He could be rude, sulky and bad tempered; he hated pain, and did not much want to say his prayers. But, as he was incurable, it needed God's grace to teach him to suffer and to die.

The first indication was generosity; he gave a pound, his collected pocket money, to have Mass said for his mother. Then he asked about maimed boys becoming priests, saying he thought he would be one. This was the chance to explain that he could do priestly work by offering his sufferings each day for other people and for particular intentions, which I gave him. He agreed. But it was difficult to tell how much he was doing, until he first refused to take the major drugs and then said to me: "I have been praying for more pain, so that I can offer it up." At this stage, he was wracked from head to foot with a cough, had intense pain in his chest, back and stomach, and his leg had swollen like a balloon. He was also covered with irritation all over, was sick each time he ate, and had a bad bedsore on his sound thigh. And then he prayed for more pain! In six months he had come from hating and resenting to accepting and offering, so that the day before he died he said: "It is a very good thing I got ill like this. I should have done much worse things had I grown up, and now I can offer the pain for what I have done wrong." He went on like that till the end, and looking up at me on the last afternoon he said: "I will pray for you in heaven."

This happened in a boy of fifteen, because he allowed himself to open to God's grace. He did not like suffering; he did not change from being a boy and having a boy's faults; but he accepted and offered. He learned that he could show his prayer and his love in suffering, even when he did not understand.

Now, we are scared to give; scared of the consequences. Yet it is urgently necessary to give immediately and openhandedly. It is oh so worth while to make life a whole in prayer, the liturgy, Mass and Communion, at work and at home.

It is a conversion, a revolution, maybe, which has to come into your life. Face it then humbly as a child, openly as a child. See the size of the task and do not be afraid, for God is with you. It is a steady climb to the summit. Well, then, the sooner you begin to climb the better, for it is up God's mountain you have to go. There is no time like the present, because there is no future. All is present in God's eternal now. Naturally you hesitate; naturally you make a query. Just as naturally you will find that the same has happened in all ages, and that is why the same is being said today as was said thousands of years ago. Man's nature is much the same, making the eternal question; but God's nature is exactly the same, and always will be, making the eternal appeal of his love. That love stands drawing all men to a cross set on a hill:

> O God, thou art my God; how eager my quest for thee,
> Body athirst and soul longing for thee, like some parched wilderness,
>   where stream is none!
> So, in the holy place, I contemplate thee, ready for the revelation of
>   thy greatness, thy glory.
> To win thy favour is dearer to me than life itself; my songs of
>   praise can no more be withheld.
> So, all my life long, I will bless thee, holding up my hands in
>   honour of thy name;
> My heart filled, as with some rich feast, my mouth in joyful accents
>   singing thy praise.[1]

[1] Ps. 62 (Knox translation).

ACKNOWLEDGEMENTS

PERMISSION to reproduce some of the articles in this book has been gratefully received, and acknowledgements are made to the following:

L.O.C.K. (*The Key*) for "Hey, You!", "What and Why," "Talking Things Over," "Daydreaming or Loving?", "Those Awful Devotions," "Recollection," and "Generosity in Prayer"; Blackfriars Publications Ltd (*The Life of the Spirit*) for "Simple Steps towards Mental Prayer", "Sharing the Sacrifice," and "The Example of Padre Pio"; *The Tablet* for "Mother of the Year".

The author also wishes to express his thanks to Miss Joan Cooley for typing out the articles.